GW01045606

To Lady Tr

A special friend

of Felicity's in THE

HOUSE OF LORDS

December 4/2008

FELICITY LANE-FOX

FELICITY LANE-FOX

Triumphing Over Disability

Felicity Lane-Fox

Book Guild Publishing
Sussex, England

First published in Great Britain in 2008 by
The Book Guild Ltd
Pavilion View
19 New Road
Brighton, BN1 1UF

Typeset in Times by
Ellipsis Books Limited, Glasgow

Printed in Great Britain by
CPI Antony Rowe

A catalogue record for this book is available from
The British Library.

ISBN 978 1 84624 274 8

Contents

1

Starters

When the polio virus strikes even the doctors tremble. Its aim is to kill or to cripple and the victims of a severe attack can be condemned to a life sentence of struggle, heartache and disillusionment. It hammered me at the age of twelve and from that moment all the physical independence I had taken for granted vanished overnight. I shudder to think how much my disability barged in to disrupt the ordinary plans and hopes of my family, for from then on I have had to depend heavily on those who are closest to me. It was their character and approach to life that reduced the handicap of my ugly disabilities, no matter if the burden nearly broke them.

My good luck was to have exceptional parents, both of whom came from Yorkshire. We lived at Walton House in the village of Walton three miles east of Wetherby and, apart from accidents and disasters, our lives there were exceedingly happy. My father, Edward Lane Fox, was retiring, kind and patient. He loved cricket, foxhunting, gardening, theatre and radio. He and my mother, Enid, were devoted to each other and both had a keen sense of humour. Enid was seventeen years younger and immensely co-ordinated, compassionate, witty and original. They provided the atmosphere which enabled us as children to participate in life to the full.

Joan, Jimmy and Prudence already occupied the nursery when I appeared and their ages then were respectively seven, six and two and three quarters. Years before I had polio I started to be a nuisance: at the age of two, an agonising right arm with a soaring temperature was diagnosed as periostitis – an infection of the covering of the bone akin to osteomyelitis. Amputation was considered and even then it was thought uncertain that I should survive, but both the limb and the day were saved by a clever surgeon who scraped the bone and rid me of the bug. He operated in Leeds and for four years after this macabre incident, frequent and diabolical dressings had to be endured while shavings of bone continued to emerge. For me, the only compensation was that my mother did the dressings and she was like magic.

At last the bandages came off and my right arm was rated fit for use, though still badly scarred from shoulder to elbow, aching a lot and very weak. It felt totally different from my left arm but I was encouraged to use it provided I took care not to bump it. All this made me a late starter, especially as I had a phobia about the doctor's car or anything that reminded me of the pain. The wise plan adopted was to try and make me forget about my arm, which must have worked for that arm was soon steering a bicycle and swinging a tennis racket. Nevertheless, I still like to blame on it my pawky performance on a pony.

Our house, built of stone in the late Georgian period, had a kind and friendly face. Three high front door steps led into a hall with dining-room and drawing-room at either side. A staircase broke at a half-landing before it reached the wide passage leading to the main bedrooms and our nurseries, from which the windows overlooked the drive and stone stable block through two large chestnut trees. The schoolroom was down the back-stairs, between pantry and kitchen. The general effect was cosy and pretty; it was not at all grand but, there was good furniture and always lovely flowers.

There was much activity in our household. Church and village meetings were held there, as well as my mother's district nursing and hospital meetings, not to mention those of the Hunt committee. Both my parents were magistrates and sat on the Wetherby bench on different days. Sunday luncheon- and tennis-parties were the norm in summer. There were also house guests who generally included our Stobart cousins – the children of my mother's sister, Esmée, and Hugo Stobart – Paul, Oliver and Simon. Simon was my age and we became the closest allies. Reinforced by the Stobarts, each year we descended on the York Fancy Dress Ball and generally returned laden with trophies as tribute to the ingenuity of my mother and her sewing-lady. My mother took great trouble about our clothes and general well-being, and excellent Nannie Holland adored her and carried out her wishes. It was hinted that Nannie spoilt me but she did not think so, and neither did I.

The Walton House garden provided grass banks to roll down, paths to bike along and a kitchen garden to raid. My father and his astute if monosyllabic gardener, Mr Farndale, created a flower garden worth anybody's viewing money, and when it was opened each year for charity it always achieved a record gate. We had great contests with the Stobarts at croquet and tennis and when my arm had improved I became a keen player, so my mother organised tennis tournaments backed up by sideshows for many neighbours of my age group. As Simon could be relied upon always to have something funny to say we usually planned for him to be there.

Every year we went to Filey with the Stobarts. As well as lots of bathing, picnicking and visiting the 'pierrots', we went deep-sea fishing with two marvellous fishermen, Councillor Jenkinson and his mate Cammish, both looking a match for all the elements. We revered them in their oilskins, huge waders and cable stitch jerseys; even if we felt sick miles out from the shore with a heavy swell running we could never lose face in front of our heroes. Filey was bliss.

Fred Shutt was in charge of the stables at Walton. He had become my father's groom ten years before my parents married – a born comedian, and skilful not only with horses but with children. The riding prowess of my sisters and brother satisfied even his standards but I only retrieved my reputation with him when I became a passable skater, for Fred was also in charge of all toboggans, hockey sticks, cricket bats, fireworks and skates.

I detested lessons in the schoolroom with our French governess and was delighted to go to a small day school in Wetherby started by Miss Wills, a fan of my mother's and a renowned educationalist. Her appearance, with hair dyed blue-black and a fringe, was against her but she quickly won my loyalty and made me keen to learn. I was in healthy awe of her and shook with apprehension every time I found, when half way to a piano lesson, I had left my music book at home.

Even before I fell prey to polio, my mother had to deal with serious health calamities in the family. Disaster struck first when my father had a bad hunting fall and was thought to have broken his neck. Days later it was discovered that the damage might be remedied if he wore a surgical collar, and when he had done so for half a year he seemed to make a complete recovery. Only a few months later, however, severe rheumatoid arthritis flared up in both hips and although deep ray treatment arrested it my father found he could no longer ride a horse nor play cricket. Fred was dismayed, declaring that for him nothing could compare with the hunting and cricket days he had shared with my father.

Disaster struck again during Jimmy's first half at Eton. He had taken a tidy place there from his prep school where he had been captain of school and of games. The Eton authorities sent for my parents to take him home with a suspected T.B. lung. He had lost pounds in weight and developed a ghastly cough. They took him to a Leeds consultant who advised that, as he would never be well enough to return, Jimmy's name should be removed from Eton. This my father flatly refused to accept. He was said to be too ill to be taken to Switzerland so, with characteristic *sangfroid*, my parents removed the windows from my father's smoking-room and turned it into a groundfloor bedroom for Jimmy. From there, my mother carried him pig-a-back to bath and loo and soon noticed that he was getting heavier. A second opinion found that the trouble never had been T.B. and that the shadows on the X-ray plates were caused by old whooping-cough scars. Jimmy returned to school and justified my father's unusually adamant decision by becoming captain of the house and achieving most available colours for games. He showed robust health for the next forty years.

My sister Prudence rode well and no-one thought it likely she would have a bad fall, but the third disaster happened one morning when we were out cub-hunting with a groom standing in for Fred, who had at last been persuaded to take a holiday. The first I knew of it was when I saw a gloomy knot of people huddled round a broken figure on the ground. Eventually an ambulance arrived to take her to Leeds where she was found to have eight fractures to her skull, a broken jaw, and a broken cheekbone; two months later, a broken neck was diagnosed. She survived through wonderful surgery and for sixteen weeks my mother stayed in Leeds to be near and help to nurse her. When they came home they brought with them a trained nurse who remained with us to keep a professional eye on Prudence for a year. The whole affair was a shattering experience for us all and it made me realise just how much I had depended on my sister, especially as we had shared the same night nursery. She was blessed with a calm temperament and, as soon as she got home and back to her dogs, of whom she was so fond, she made and sustained steady progress to almost complete recovery. After a year she was back at lessons, sailed through her school certificate and started to ride again.

The hard frost of 1929 provided us with a skating rink on nearby floodwater where we held ice-hockey matches and I was allowed to keep goal. Joan's many friends and admirers included some dashing skaters and I became so absorbed that it was difficult to get down to school homework, which had usually given me no trouble. The ice soon disappeared in the spring, the buttercups glistened in the sunshine and the larks sang in the sky. Life felt full and free, secure and kindly, and on our way to visit Jimmy at school my mother took me for one packed morning's sightseeing in London. The Tower, Westminster Abbey, Buckingham Palace, Cleopatra's Needle and Madame Tussaud's left me forever enchanted by the metropolis.

My private plans were not to settle down and marry when I grew up but seek an ambitious career. The life of either an actress or a barrister appealed to me, but this was aiming high and in my less ebullient moments I toyed with the thought of becoming a nun. First, however, I had to go away to school and this was arranged to happen in six months' time. Having heard my mother's accounts of her happy and successful school career at Roedean I had no doubt that Westonbirt, in Wiltshire, would be entirely to my liking. Just to think about the uniform was thrilling and I was rather pleased to be tall for my age at five foot seven inches when I was only twelve. It was all very exciting and I could hardly wait.

2

Body Blow

For domestic reasons the customary hordes of us did not go to Filey in 1930. Instead, Prudence and I were sent there for one week, accompanied by the nurse who had looked after her and who could deal with the headaches which were the only after-effects of her fall. We went to the most reasonably priced rooms available at the Royal Crescent Hotel and my mother brought Simon over for the day to settle us in. We bathed in the sea and had a lovely time, but I had a bit of a stiff neck and, coming up the hill from the beach, found it a struggle to drag my legs along, which was unusual. At lunch, when somebody ragged me I burst into hot tears in the middle of the public dining-room and this also was untypical, but when Joan visited us later that day with one of the dashing skaters, Percy Legard, I busily accompanied them to the Brigg. There we got caught in a cloud-burst and I sheltered with Percy under a rock and his coat.

Half way through the night I woke up, nipped out of bed to go to the loo and found my legs heavy and unwilling to walk. Suddenly, they collapsed under me and sent me sprawling on the red and blue turkey carpet on the corridor. Puzzled, I picked myself up and got back into bed where I promptly went off to sleep again. Next day I was kept in bed. Simon came over and he and Prudence stayed with me most of the day in my tiny room, though I was too drowsy to care.

My temperature had soared by next day and the local practitioner, Dr Simpson, was called. Sensing his concern, Prudence telephoned my mother to say she felt sure I was seriously ill. By the time my mother arrived polio had been diagnosed and confirmed; mine turned out to be the only case notified in North Yorkshire that autumn. By a coincidence, Dr Simpson's daughter had been a polio victim a few years earlier and, although her attack was slight and she had soon recovered, he was quick to spot the symptoms again. With Dr Simpson's agreement, my mother contacted Sir Robert Jones who was then the authority on this foul disease. He promised to come all the way over from Liverpool, insisting that he must first have measurements of my back, and the size of my hands and feet, for his splintmaker.

Although everything hurt abominably, I felt much better just to see my mother. It caused me excruciating pain to be moved at all and even the muscles in my face caused agony. I talked more incessantly than was my wont, until my breathing needed to be helped; talk then became impossible. Sleep was out of the question. There was no difference between night and day. My inside seized up and there came a time when everybody's attention was fixed on whether or not I could 'spend a penny'. Nothing could be too calamitous if my mother was with me, so her and Dr Simpson's visits provided the only recognisable rays of hope. In my left leg and sciatic nerve the pain was outrageous and sweat poured off me from sheer agony.

After three days Sir Robert Jones arrived, his white hair and moustache and blue eyes sparkling above his white coat. I liked him, but not his splints. I strongly objected to the leather and iron backsplint which made the bedpan still less inviting, and the hand and feet splints were like chain mail. On top of all the pain, this seemed just too much. In our family we never talked about anything so 'wet' as nerves, but now everything tore at mine, particularly the noise of the sea and the sight of the nurses. It was one long, ghastly nightmare.

Brave Dr Simpson decided that, with the help of a colleague, he could plaster one foot to get the same effect as Sir Robert's steel splint and with less discomfort. Even when the pain was eased the whole area of my foot tickled acutely and my mother spent long hours obeying my urgent directions to ease my discomfort – 'A bit left; no, a bit right!' – until she must have been totally exhausted.

The hotel agreed that my bed could be gingerly moved into a larger room next door and a second nurse was installed. As Prudence's nurse was with us when I got ill, she remained, though she found me an unco-operative patient compared with Prudence. In return, I found her a tedious bore! Yet in my case, no less than in Prudence's, it was careful nursing which provided the one chance of preserving dwindling life. With elbows bent and splinted, my arms were tied to the bedhead, hands and fingers bent round splints. Because I was so thin my prominent hip bones were rubbed with spirit continuously to stop them breaking through the skin. All 'ruderies', such as enemas hurt abominably because of the inflamed nerves.

When other hotel guests were evacuated from the dangerous area of infection the financial loss had to be made good by my family, whose small resources were already heavily strained. People who had been friendly with us before, now hated the sight of us and when they saw my mother and Prudence out for a breath of air in the street hurried across to the other side. Who could blame them?

For a time even my mother could get no positive response from me. Eating was of no interest and in desperation she recalled my deep-seated love of adornment. I had told her touching tales of gazing for days in a shop window where two bone bracelets were priced too high for my pocket money, so the bracelets were now purchased and forced down over my hand splints. She pandered to my vanity by combing my hair and tying it up in ribbons; she even varnished my fingernails on their splints. The worst of the pain began to recede after ten days and, although the discomfort was still acute, at least I was aware of what was happening and even realised that Prudence had gone home to be replaced by my father. His dislike of the seaside was notorious and to know that he had driven himself over in the Baby Austin (which he had only recently learnt to drive) made me feel flattered and important. A few days later Joan called in and began to read me *The Good Companions*, which I loved, and my health soon improved accordingly.

A few other faithful allies visited us, despite the residual risk, including Paul Stobart, who hated illness but appeared to have appreciated in his young mind the drama and anguish of our situation. Another visitor was my mother's spinster aunt, Maria Bethell, aged ninety. A touching pair of callers were the two fishermen, Jenks and Cammish; kings of the sea in our eyes, now they stood by my bedside in their best dark blue jerseys twiddling their caps in salty, gnarled hands, looking pathetically sad and helpless.

Eating was a horror and for four weeks I could take only glucose and malt extracts. Then my mother somehow persuaded me to eat sweetbreads in white sauce, followed next day by a tutti-frutti ice cream, the name of which seemed so funny that I had to eat it. Gradually these battles grew less. Outsiders helped to raise my spirits with letters that made fun of my predicament and treated it as nothing out of the ordinary. Percy Legard drew caricatures of what he thought I must look like all strung up on splints, and someone wrote to ask what on earth I thought I was doing, staying on in Filey when all the donkeys were in their winter dustsheets. Simon sent a strange parcel of fir cones, because he had found them in a wood and thought they smelt nice. My godfather sent us an elaborate reading desk, but it needed someone to turn the pages and my eyes hurt to read; in the past I had seldom been still long enough to read a book for pleasure.

Dr Simpson had an interest in home and international politics and loved to talk about them. He must have seen a faint glint of interest in my eye so a wireless was fixed up and I began to get news of political situations. My mother and I attempted to harmonise current songs and older ones that she taught me. We gave at least spirited renderings of 'On the Sunny Side of the Street', 'Without a Song', and 'Kitty, Kitty'. Despite my very frail condition, at last plans were made to get me home. Both the hotel proprietors and the doctor could not have been more delighted to be getting rid of us but, after the last six weeks of captivity, our delight was greater than theirs.

I tried, surreptitiously, to extract important information from my mother before we left Filey. Knowing a family friend who had succumbed to recurrent attacks of malaria, I asked if my 'chill-thing' was likely to recur? Her answer was that she jolly well hoped *not*, so I gathered that this had been something serious and I asked if the doctors knew what it was? She cleverly avoided making any reference to infantile paralysis, the effects of which she knew I understood, and said I had had 'poliomyelitis', knowing that I had not heard of it and would be pleased with the smart long name.

The ambulance men put me gingerly on the stretcher and carried me down the hotel passage. I could see the red and blue turkey carpet and remembered the night my legs had let me down. There was a mawkish clutch of onlookers gathered round the hotel entrance but just when I hoped to impress both them and the ambulance men my head turned swimmy. The fifty mile journey seemed endless for there were several stops on the way. At last we swung round on to the crunch of the Walton House gravel drive and through the ambulance window I could just see the chestnut trees, by now a bit bedraggled. Familiar voices, muffled and awestruck, reached my ears; my father, Fred, Farndale, Maurice, Alfred were assembled to help with the stretcher. Immediately I felt stronger, which illustrates that when the acute stage has passed, ordinary, favourite things have a therapeutic value far greater than the best nursing.

I had never expected those three front door steps and two flights of stairs would create such obstacles to our progress. In the past they had just been something to fly up and down but now they presented mountainous difficulties. Urging the stretcher through the door into my room also produced an ugly struggle, followed by a breathless scrimmage to get it, and me, onto my bed. I could not move my head but my eyes peered round and were not pleased with what they saw. My bed was newly positioned in the middle of the room, and for this I blamed the nurses. At least I could see the trees through the window, and when the door handle turned it made the same old noise. To my chagrin what I thought of as the nursing palaver had returned with us, but at least I now had the measure of my surroundings. Uncharitably, I hoped to disappoint the nurses by saying I felt perfectly well, implying that they could take their skills elsewhere. My mother smoothed this over by saying she always knew I had been a humbug.

Our household was going to be stuffed with nurses and, as Nannie would be quite out of her element both with me in this state and with them, my mother had the rotten task of persuading her to take a job with well children where her talents would have full scope. Strangely, this was a relief to me, perhaps because it was always hard for Nannie to disguise her feelings. What I wanted now was to talk about ordinary, humdrum things, to hear mild gossip and get to know what was going on. I was very interested to hear about everyone who had skated with us and any news about where and with whom they had been seen soon satisfied my eager curiosity. This, added to my mother's powers of entertainment, greatly diminished the nursing horrors.

My parents decided to stick to the Filey doctor who had served us so well, as his attentions were now rarely required. My mother and two sisters had quickly learnt to shift me in bed and my mother had adapted Sir Robert Jones' unbending variety of mattress to make the middle section removable, which simplified the bedpan problem out of all recognition. Before, to be lifted on and off the bedpan had been dreadfully painful, but now it was not nearly so bad. A stage developed when I much preferred everything to be done for me by anyone other than a nurse, and this especially applied to being fed. I hated every spoonful offered to me by a nurse and, though I tried to be polite, anything they did with me seemed to have the kiss of death. By November one nurse had been eased away and before Christmas Prudence's old nurse had gone for a prolonged change. I am ashamed to say that this was the most welcome Christmas present I had ever received.

Once a day my helpless hands were taken off their splints and it was then we were reminded that both hands and arms were virtually good for nothing. Nobody seemed quite sure what to do with them and when my mother tried repeatedly moving them for me she elicited no response whatever. Somehow, in her inimitable way, she turned it into a joke. Meanwhile my legs and feet got sore and were constantly nipped by their splints, so needed to be rubbed and moved about in one way or another. My right foot was the most active limb but would try to break its bonds by pointing downwards, which we were told must cause trouble for the future. At last we could plan further than from day to day and my mother was told of a 'first-class Swedish masseuse' in Leeds, with a daughter who was newly qualified in physiotherapy and physical education. The fact that their name was Rudé delighted me.

Dr Simpson came over to discuss my case with Madame and Miss Rudé and in no time I had fallen completely for these delightful Scandinavians. They wore white overalls, yes, but they were smilingly healthy individuals who had no morbid preoccupation with illness. The daughter was called Monna. Once they had agreed on a routine to be followed they arranged to come out the sixteen miles from Leeds three times a week until I became strong enough to go to them. Soon I felt that Monna, like my mother, was a force tugging me back into the fun of life. She seemed certain that all she did for me was right and soon won my confidence. Madame, with her fascinating pidgin-English, waged war on my left elbow where the muscles were contracted and soon got it almost straight, while Monna dealt firmly with my errant right foot. She fired instructions at me in gorgeous, velvety tones and I responded to the utmost.

In these circumstances I improved rapidly. It was decided to get me up and carry me downstairs on a stretcher and there transfer me to a long wicker chair which had been touchingly bought for me by Prudence. Always conscious of the expense her own calamity had cost the family, she had set up an agency in the village for selling Indian tea to supplement her pocket money. She had found this semi-garden chair through a newspaper advertisement and produced it without anybody knowing. To follow medical instructions my arms had to be propped with cushions to keep them level with my shoulders, and I had to lie almost flat with my legs stretched straight out ahead. To me my arms and legs felt weightless but to everyone else they weighed a ton. They fell helplessly off the stretcher or off the chair and took ages to arrange, but despite these preparations it was wonderful to be downstairs. Stretcher bearers were required at 11.00 a.m. and 3.30 p.m. and it was not always easy to get the four needed at just these times. The lion's share was taken by my mother, Fred and Maurice, the young butler. It had quickly been discovered that every time my father helped to carry, his back and hip seized up and as this made two cripples instead of one, he was strictly forbidden to touch the stretcher. Nevertheless, my mother firmly insists that she could not have surmounted the difficulties and heartbreaks of the first year without my father, and even I could feel that his serene personality was a strong, sure influence behind all the activity.

The next step was to get me out of doors, so Joan went to Carters in London and found a lavishly upholstered long, outdoor chair, to be drawn by either a person or a pony. It cost my parents the then astronomical sum of £100. It was sumptuously comfortable with plenty of space to prop up my helpless arms at the required angle. Just to be outside and able to look at the trees and sky made me feel better. My present situation still seemed totally unreal, like some prolonged and not very pleasant charade, and I half expected that it would soon all come right. In my dreams at night I still raced about the garden and could remember just how it felt to run about on the lawn and up the steps. Nevertheless it was marvellous just to see it all for myself again.

Dr Simpson suggested that for part of the time I was outside my chair be pushed to a corner of the garden where I was out of ear-shot. He said life would require me to develop inner resources and he considered that I should be encouraged to do so now. They wheeled me to where I could be seen but not converse and I felt as though I had been sent to Coventry. My parents put up a bird table in the hope that this would interest me, but only the sparrows used it. One complication in the long chair was finding a way to give me a bedpan. Even when a solution was discovered it still meant that I slipped down in the chair each time it was used and had to be hauled up again, making it an undertaking which called for several helpers. What made it worse was my perfectly maddening modesty. My chair would be dragged round into the garage and all the doors closed, but if an outsider had the least suspicion of what we were doing I nearly had a fit. Should anyone unwittingly come to the door before we were ready, I was upset for hours and nothing my mother said would soothe me.

When Sir Robert Jones came to stay the night to inspect his patient in conference with Dr Simpson, they were clearly very pleased. I was much stronger and no longer needed to be regarded as a delicate creature. Our bitter disappointment was that he had no magic formula to get us out of all this. He did not disguise the fact that he took a dim view of my spine and shoulder muscles and even told my parents that it was unlikely I should ever be able to sit up again, feed myself or even scratch my own nose. Undeterred, my mother made his visit worth his while by taking him to see the local home for crippled children, which he was pleased with, and Leeds General Infirmary, which he considered needed blowing up! He told me the story of how the famous Sister Agnes was given by King Edward VII a special key to the garden of Buckingham Palace to enable her to take a short cut to her hospital in London. Sir Robert and Sister Agnes had worked together for years at the Oswestry Orthopaedic Hospital and were dedicated to improving things for people with orthopaedic conditions. The result was the emergence of brilliant young doctors like Mr Girdlestone, who went on to make an illustrious name at Oxford's Wingfield Orthopaedic Hospital. To hear how many other people had to be immobilised and on splints helped me to put my own situation in better perspective.

Because Liverpool and Sir Robert were so far away, a local consultant was called in. Mr Daw, the father of one of Miss Wills' pupils, although a gifted doctor, was himself so badly crippled by arthritis that it took him nearly half an hour to climb our stairs. When he examined my right foot and made the ominous comment 'We must bend it up by fair means or foul', I secretly wondered if this was to be his revenge on our stairs. The remark seemed the more sinister as the poor old boy was bent almost double himself, but at least it was useful to Monna who reminded me of what he had said if ever I resisted her attempts to loosen my foot and ankle. To be with Monna was so much to my liking that even to be disentangled by her was not unpleasant.

Mr Daw suggested that for the daily exercising of my limbs we have slings from a Balkan beam. While Monna was quite in favour of it, she saw that this would take a lot of fixing up and organising. With the help of the local carpenter, posts were placed at each end of my bed and fitted with rings to which slings could be attached. As *we* had to make the slings, my mother rushed to the local haberdashery to buy yards of strong calico. When all was ready my arms were first placed in the slings, then my legs.

Almost immediately one frail arm after another slipped away, followed by my left leg, whereas its companion kicked merrily downwards in the direction nobody wished it to go, virtually pulling down that part of this infuriating contraption. We persevered until my arms and legs were sore from the slings and other people's arms and legs were exhausted from retrieving my fall-outs. After one week we learnt from Monna how to achieve the same degree of exercise without the slings and we all worked away to make sure we got good results before Mr Daw's next visit.

Although the beam posts had greatly hindered my mother and her helpers in nursing, bedbathing and dressing me, she now designed a stretcher with which three people could put me into the bath. It was made of rubberised canvas and had holes cut in it to let the water out. Holding three sets of leather handles at each side, the carriers could lower me into the water, with some trepidation but not much difficulty. I found this thrilling.

That winter, it was decided to take me to the pantomime at the Leeds Theatre Royal. The local Black Maria was the only vehicle that could transport me on my wicker chair. The driver was suitably lugubrious, having an enormous black moustache, and it made an exciting drive to know that this was how the pickpockets were shipped off from the Wetherby racecourse. The afternoon was going splendidly until I discovered that someone had brought a bedpan. This spelt both insult and ignominy. It was only when I had extracted a promise that in no circumstances would it be brought out of hiding that I could enjoy the afternoon. Because of my chair we were in a ground floor box and from my recumbent position it was pretty difficult to see the stage at all. However, it felt marvellous to be there, particularly when Cora Goffin, the principal boy, sent round chocolates in a golden box.

Our Lane Fox cousins at Bramham Park lent us a pony called Fairy, used to working between the shafts of a pony-cart, in order to pull my chair so that we might go further afield. My mother now gave up hunting and walked miles with my chair. That year the skies would suddenly darken with great flocks of hundreds of thousands of starlings which generally contrived to escort us home from all our expeditions. To me this was just one more unexpected phenomenon symbolic of this strange fantasy through which we were passing.

It was a revelation to see the reactions to my present situation of old friends of my age. Simon picked up again exactly where we left off, and not only did he write to me every week but he tried to engineer other ways to include me. His worst difficulty here was that, although his family had moved from County Durham to be much nearer to Walton at Middlethorpe, their dear old Queen Anne house had a very stiff flight of front door steps and a playroom for the children in the basement. Other friends were more fickle than Simon, for they remembered me as particularly active and fairly vigorous, whereas they now saw me frail and wan, covered in apparatus and under the anxious eye of my mother. It appeared to be more than they could take and they tended to fade away.

This was not at all the case with my brother, sisters and cousins. Prudence, Joan and Jimmy showed no embarrasment and behaved as though nothing odd had happened, sharing the burden of my misfortune almost as though it were their own and appearing to take it very much for granted. They and Simon played endless verbal contests with me – spelling bees, animal-vegetable-mineral and the geography game. Most important of all they did not treat me as a delicate object but as a normal individual, temporarily swathed in inconvenient splints and equipment. Secretly, I minded terribly about being unable to use my hands to play draughts, halma, peggity, and, worse still, to turn the gramophone on and off. Thoughts of tennis, the swing and hammock, the bicycle and dancing, were now in a category of longings as remote as going to the moon. But these were unspoken sadnesses because we were all together in this mess and I did not want to make a fuss to let the others down.

My mother made endless enquiries for the best equipment available to get me into a car. What she found was a complete blank. Monna's efforts had made me able to bear my legs being hung down from the knee, so my mother designed a second stretcher, made in canvas by the saddler, to enable me to be lifted into the front seat of a car. To get me into the back seat at first seemed a more likely proposition but proved impossible because the lifters' arms were never long enough. On the whole our method worked out well, though I had to be tied into the seat because I flopped about. The great thing was that I could now go to Leeds for treatment with Monna. Either my mother and Fred, or one of them and a helper, accompanied me there and helped Monna to carry me up the steps into their cheerful gymnasium with its remedial plinth and electrical machines.

Monna soon became very dashing in evolving ways to move me about, and even hauled me up onto my feet in front of her. As I had grown by four inches to five foot, eleven inches while laid up in bed it now felt as though I was looking down a mountainside. Prompted by Monna, the doctor prescribed a full-length, weight-bearing caliper splint and when, after the long weeks it took to make, the splintmaker brought it to Monna's and put it on, Monna found that by getting me onto my feet and walking backwards in front of me I was enabled to take a few steps. The splintmaker exclaimed delightedly: 'She will go! She will go!' I thought wryly that it was all very well for him to talk like that . . .

My hands had begun to respond to treatment and the fingers had straightened out. The right hand was clearly the less helpless of the two but as the biceps on that arm were practically non-existent, having been more than normally affected on account of the large chunk of muscle removed in treating the periostitis, the arm refused to lift or bend from the elbow without assistance. Paradoxically, while the left hand was disinclined to move even a finger, my left biceps were pretty useful and would sometimes help my right arm. While my right triceps would operate very slightly, my left triceps were virtually absent. I still could not hold anything in either hand nor feed myself.

In all our activities my mother remained aware of Sir Robert's advice, that as I was so tall it was very necessary not to overtire recovering muscles. At first he had been doubtful whether treatment on three days a week would not be too much, but it was not long before my mother became as convinced as I that Monna knew exactly what was the best for me. My physio. sessions were very strenuous and exercised all groups of muscles affected – which meant the lot. Much time was spent face down on the plinth in an effort to bring back into action my gluteal, hamstring and quadricep muscles. Soon my right leg got much stronger in bending backwards and pressing down when straight, but it never regained the ability to lift itself forwards and the weak ankle muscles remained a deadly trap in a leg needed as a reliable prop. As for my left leg it boringly showed only the tiniest flicker of muscle response to Monna's consistently determined efforts, yet she insisted that, when my walking exercises were over, the caliper be removed to allow every chance for the muscles to improve. My back and spine made wonderful progress and soon allowed me to be sat up quite stably without any support. While that was more than Sir Robert had predicted, he proved to be horribly right about my deltoids.

With no shoulder muscles to lift your arms either up or out from your sides, you are extremely handicapped. By the time I had fallen over once or twice it was soon recognised that I could do nothing whatever to save myself from falling, having no arm to stretch out. Because I could put no weight on my stupidly frail arms, no sticks, crutches or walking-frames were of the slightest help. Largely through the philosophically light-hearted approach adopted by Monna, I was able to make all these dreary discoveries without feeling too desperate, and in the eight years I went to her for treatment I never once regretted having to go.

At night, it was quite impossible for me to move my position in bed so another bed was put into my room and occupied by my mother or, on a very few occasions, by Prudence. I used to wake up stiff and aching and often needed to be shifted twice a night. My mother made every conceivable adaptation to make dressing easier but even so the business of threading clumsily helpless arms and legs in and out of sleeves and stockings, for instance, was both tricky and exhausting. It was hard to cater for practical matters, such as coping with the loo despite trousers, especially as I was obstinately opposed to wearing anything that was obviously adapted and always longed for elegant clothes. In one way or another my mother generally produced garments that met with my approval, but her task was made no easier by sudden medical decisions. When she had just introduced a new method for dressing me so that I could sit up, the doctors found something suspicious about my spine and ordered me to lie down flat again. After a few hysterical days they decided that what they had found was only a harmless irregularity, so our old technique was again resumed.

Finding stretcher bearers for the stairs morning and night became too much and my mother scoured the shops in London and the north for some other means of moving me, without success. So we accepted the kind offer of our elderly neighbour, Sir Edward Brooksbank, to lend us his old-fashioned upright wooden chair which had a wicker seat, four small wheels and two well placed handles for pulling it up steps. Now we could tackle the stairs with one strong person at the back and another crouched in front to give an extra shove. After a time, Maurice became so adept that he could pull the chair up both flights singlehanded and at the double. For long periods my legs were kept in an elevated position, so a detachable foot-rest was added to the chair and it now became much more of a favourite with me than the long, upholstered version. In this one it was possible to be pulled up the front doorsteps without needing to be unshipped, which gave it a definite edge of popularity over the other model. Mamma decided that now was the moment to dispose of the long chair but was amazed to hear from the suppliers that they would offer only £10 and had no other suggestion for its disposal. We all felt very bitter and my parents decided to keep the vehicle to lend to other unfortunates similarly handicapped.

In the following years the chair was lent to several individuals who were having mobility troubles, and in 1946 I was introduced to a girl called Susan Armstrong-Jones, the daughter of Lady Rosse and the niece of Oliver Messel. She said that her younger brother, Tony, had returned from Eton badly smitten by polio and that they were anxious to find a means of getting him into the garden, the more so because he was deeply interested in photography. This was obviously a job for my long chair which was still in mint condition, so we sent it off there. Whether it was used or not I do not know, for in four months it was returned with a note from Susan to say that her brother was making a miraculous recovery and no longer needed a chair of any kind.

My brother was chosen to play in the Eton XI at Lord's in 1931 and the fact that he was only to be twelfth man was not divulged to him or us before Sir Pelham ('Plum') Warner, an old cricketing friend of my father's, had offered to lend us his box so that I could be included in this great family occasion. To get me to London was no small undertaking but, game as ever, my parents took me by car to Flemings Hotel in Clarges Street. Fred drove the car and a helper preceded us by train with the luggage. The Brooksbank chair travelled on the carrier of the car and caused quite a stir when it was set up on the pavement by Fred, who made encouraging hissing noises, as though in the stables. We then began the inelegant business of transferring me from car to chair, not helped at all by a very high kerb and a difficult front doorstop with overhanging lip, surmounted by a heavy swingdoor. The next discovery was that the chair would only just fit into the lift, while on the bedroom floor there were three nasty steps to negotiate in order to reach our rooms. These obstacles, however, were nothing to compare with those which faced us when we tried to get the chair into the box at Lord's. Kindly people dressed up in their best – and the wonderful Fred, hissing hard – heaved desperately at the stretcher to persuade it round the winding stair in order to place me on the *chaise longue* set out in readiness. The trouble was that when at last they got me into position there was no hope whatever of seeing over the edge of the box. Fortunately, Jimmy was a substitute fieldsman for a bit, so we were able to cheer when he ran for a ball. I had a sneaking suspicion that the commotion I caused spoilt a lot of the family's fun.

That was not all there was to the London trip. There were three lovely bonuses and one dreadful snag. The first bonus was that Nannie Holland called on us from her new job in the metropolis, reminding us of her charms and convincing both herself and us that she could not have stood the strain of our current predicament. The second bonus was that I met for the first time my godfather and fell for him, only regretting that he had not seen me before I became a physical wreck, and feeling that it was hard luck on him to be saddled with damaged goods. The last bonus was to see for a moment Percy Legard, who admitted he had been terrified of contracting polio from me. Those were the bonuses. The snag was Mr Hickson.

A few months earlier my mother had sprung on me a leading faith healer called Hickson who came to stay at Walton as a result of pressure from well-meaning friends. I took an instant dislike to him. He had a wart on his nose and was rather stout, but that alone was not enough. I did not like his kneeling down beside me, and particularly objected to his calling a prayer session in the drawing-room, about which my chief memory is of Joan, kneeling neatly almost in the fireplace, in danger of scratching the toes of her pretty shoes. For once I wished I were not the centre of attention, and was at a loss to know quite what was expected of me. Everything seemed exactly the same when the session was over, apart from my morale which had dropped like a stone. Next morning, Mr Hickson came to my bedside to suggest that my left leg was more active now than it had been the day before and I was incensed, but I was too awestruck to tell him that I did not believe him for it was not. My mother was clearly displeased with my attitude towards the whole affair but somehow glossed over it. What I had not expected was that I should be faced with the same man again in London. At least, I should have been faced with him if I had not bellowed hysterically so long and loud that poor Mr Hickson had to be prevented from entering my room. So I returned to Walton in disgrace. The general feeling was that I was not helping myself while everyone else was bursting themselves on my behalf. When I told Monna all about it I half hoped that she would disapprove of the whole episode but soon found I was wrong. Indeed, at first she too was suitably reproving, until she collapsed with laughter to think of my churlish demonstration.

At last my hands began to show definite signs of life, much encouraged no doubts by my wish to feed myself again. My right hand still would not raise itself unaided, but my left hand could help. Our excellent food quickly transformed me from being frail and thin to a normal weight. The tragedy was that my weight did not stop there; it went on increasing. The great thing was that nobody any longer regarded me as ill, so looking after me was not now a question of nursing but of providing muscle power and general care. My right hand began to look as if it might hold a pencil, even though at first it could do no more than make a crazy squiggle. Good Miss Wills came out on the bus from Wetherby to read me literature and European history, but I was not very receptive and found it hard to concentrate when unable to take notes.

Miss Wills suggested we might like to try and take me to join her class. On the appointed day I was very excited about it, but there were many hazards to be overcome that I had not noticed before, like the steps formerly unnoticed, and the fact that there was not enough room in the hall for the chair without removing the hatstand, which meant that the poor old 'Brooksbank' was thoroughly thwarted at every turn. Any alteration to the well-known setting looked like sacrilege to me, but in her keenness to help Miss Wills seemed prepared even to pull down a wall. It proved very difficult to get me into the classroom because of the piano; as this problem was being discussed I tried to avoid the eye of Miss Wills, remembering that oft forgotten music book. Once in place my wheelchair took up most of one side of the table which normally accommodated three pupils. As a result of our invasion the day's lesson time was cut by over an hour and to get us out again took nearly as long. The experiment had not been a success so Miss Wills resumed her visits to Walton and her classes were supplemented by a teacher of elocution, a subject I enjoyed, and by a gentleman to coach me in elementary book-keeping and accountancy. My pocket money had just been replaced by a more generous allowance of £28 per year, paid in quarterly instalments of £7 each, and that gave me something to practise on.

At this time we had a visit from a friend called Gavin Fairfax who had a mis-shapen arm. Because he was in the car trade he knew of a secondhand electrically propelled invalid tricycle and wondered if it would do for me. My parents, Monna and the doctor decided that, if my hands could manage it, I could gain so much from independence by this means that it would be worth letting my legs down and even taking my arms off props. Nobody really expected me to be able to drive the chair, which looked unprepossessing and difficult to get into. I had to be lowered into the seat from above because there was no side door. To everyone's amazement, including my own, within half an hour I was dashing about up and down the garden path. The difficulty was to make me agree to get out of it. The whole venture was a resounding success and over the next weeks my arms and hands improved amazingly from driving about. My left hand became proficient in steering the spade handle attached to the column from the small front wheel and my right hand looked after the speed control and brake. The driving improved my limbs but did still more for my attitude of mind.

The village shop was now nicely within my radius of travel and I could make my own purchases again, meet and talk to people on my own and have the thrill of free-wheeling hell-for-leather down the village street. We were off! From the first day I encountered the chair until 1939, I spent a great deal of my life belting round in it. At first there were errands to be run in Wetherby and Boston Spa. Later, from the ages of fifteen to thirty-one, I paid visits to every race meeting on Wetherby Racecourse. The chair would break down, the batteries run out, and one day I was towed home behind a friendly car but the vitally important thing was that this vehicle gave me a chance for adventure, unspoilt by health limitations. Fortunately, we all remained in blissful ignorance of the fact that I needed a driving licence to take the chair on the road, until I became a county councillor sixteen years later. When I then took my test nobody could understand why I was such a proficient driver.

In order to extend our range of travel, a local horsebox driver would give the chair a lift to the Harrogate horse shows and local point-to-points. Neighbours invited me to join the chatting onlookers at their Sunday tennis-parties and on one occasion I was so absorbed in conversation sitting at the top of the garden steps that I failed to notice the twelve-year-old son of the house fiddling with the chair's controls. Suddenly we took off and charged down the steps, turning upside down at the bottom. I was told later that I fired a volley of oaths from beneath the chair, but this did not deter the other guests who showed remarkable strength and resource and lifted the ton weight off me. Both I and the chair were quite unharmed.

Swimming-pools then were very rare in Yorkshire and none of our friends had one. But Monna decided that swimming would be good for me and arranged for me to go to the Leeds municipal baths at Armley during the lunch hour. To strip me and persuade my limbs into a bathing-dress in the confines of a cubicle was no easy job, but at last we emerged and I was edged over to the side of the bath, hoping and praying that the improvement in my left leg would be enough to support me without a splint. It was nervous work. Monna went into the swimming-bath to receive me and my mother somehow lowered my huge form over the side. Immediately it hit water my left leg floated to the top through lack of muscle power and we spent a lot of time exercising it by trying to make it touch the bottom. We had more success floating me on my back and I enjoyed the freedom of movement the water allowed. We kept up the routine for the better part of a year, but that extra dressing and undressing looked likely to wear out my mother before the swimming did me much good, so we desisted. My next swimming exercises were in 1971 at the Middlesex Hospital in London, where the hydraulic lift and helpers for dressing made it all much easier.

Someone who had had polio told us of the great benefit he received from riding therapy, for in those early days 'riding for the disabled' had not been heard of. A suitably staid cob was found and new riding pants and coat were made for me. How to get me on was the poser; we decided that a roomier launching-pad than the mounting-block was needed to accommodate sundry helpers pressed into service for this occasion, so Fred led the pony on to the croquet lawn below the terrace outside the drawing-room window and I was lowered from the terrace into the saddle. My hands by then could support the reins but there was no power in either arm so this, really, was only for show. My legs slumped ridiculously out from the knee and the left one had to be permanently held in place by someone walking alongside. Feeling an awful fool, with Fred leading the cob and my mother beside me, we set off. If my steed so much as pricked its ears my balance went and I had to be grabbed firmly by the backside, but that was not enough. More helpers were required, and with Fred at the helm there was no hanging about. In the middle of nowhere the pony took fright when someone let off a gun several fields away so I all but fell off and we suddenly realised that if I did it would be extremely difficult to find a way to pick me up and transport me home. Because of my arms I could not hang on to anyone and to lift my considerable weight like a bundle into the saddle would be out of the question. This first outing taught us that, while I found it exhilarating once more to see people and places from a pony's back, this was a pretty cumbersome form of exercise which was also highly extravagant in terms of manpower. No doubt it would be wonderful, I thought, for someone short of confidence and with no electric chair, but neither of these conditions applied to me. I was glad when the experiment ended.

Friends of the family pressed my mother to take me away from Walton for a break in the summer to stay in their bungalow in the garden of their house at Bembridge on the Isle of Wight. It was a great undertaking to transport chairs, splints, stretchers and bedpans, but through a miracle of organisation, and the thoughtfulness of neighbours who lent a van to take a great deal of our paraphernalia, it worked perfectly. The van went off and we followed, driven by Fred in the car and preceded by two helpers. Aunt Esmée came down for part of the six weeks and Joan was also there, which must have been a relief for my mother who would otherwise have been saddled with my ton weight. Once we had planned a routine we were happy. I was able to watch some sizzling tennis and all the bathing beauties disporting themselves under a blazing sun.

One afternoon at Bembridge my euphoria was dismissed by a

demon cloud of reality. A friend who came to chat with my mother said that her cousin had just contracted infantile paralysis and added, '. . . just like Felicity.' I waited in vain for my mother to correct her, but she did not. I was quite stunned. Surely what I had contracted was this rare disease called poliomyelitis? Other people had infantile paralysis and that was a dreaded condition. For instance, Fred's nephew had had to wear a pot leg on account of it and there was that young woman in a bathchair when we went to Sidmouth, whose keeper I was always pestering to let me help her to get the chair up the kerbs. When I cast a covert look at my mother's face I found there no surprise. Suddenly I had a sickening thought . . . Could my thing possibly be that clumsy, unattractive, rotten infantile paralysis? My mind was in a turmoil and I could hardly wait for our guest to leave.

My mother seemed prepared for my battery of questions. She explained that polio was the American name for infantile paralysis and that as – apart from Sir Robert Jones – the Americans were more advanced than we were about it on account of President Roosevelt, she thought we would do well to follow their lead at least in regard to the name. While I was still reeling from the shock she began to talk to me for the first time about where we had got to and where we were going. She believed we had already passed a lot of milestones – Filey, finding Monna, learning to feed myself, to stand, to hold a pencil, the electric chair, getting into a car – and she said she was convinced we should find a way to manage most things. It was going to be a terrific challenge but she made it clear that *she* would not falter.

3

Climbing Back

Try as she would, my mother could not make me do my exercises with her. To this day I am not certain why this was, though it may have been through a deep-seated wish not to rub in that my progress still fell far short of what we both wanted. Outwardly, it looked cussed and unco-operative on my part. My strangely insecure walking was coming along quite well and consisted of swinging my left foot forward in its stiffened caliper and then shifting my weight across onto it. The difficulty was to prevent my far from stable right foot from tripping me up, knowing as we did that once I started to fall somebody must move like lightning to save me from hitting the floor. Good catchers, apart from Monna and my mother, were Pooh – our new name for Prudence, based on her love for Winnie the Pooh – Joan, Simon, Jimmy and Fred.

Monna devised a new method to enable one person to pull me up steps. The helper had to face me from the bottom step, catch hold of my right hand to keep the flail arm out of the way, put their right arm round my waist as if to break into a foxtrot, support me enough to lean over and get my right foot on the step, and then help to swing up my left leg. With practice we got good enough at this delicate performance to tackle a flight of stairs. It required split-second timing and I doubt if many onlookers realised how precarious we were when my mother and I regularly climbed the Walton House stairs. It was a daunting feat twice a day, but we escaped unharmed. I practised walking and stair-climbing with Monna and quite often with Simon, by now a giant at six foot, four inches, who made little of carrying my eleven stone. Joan had introduced to us Bill and Tony Yates, who both became amazingly willing and strong lifters for me. They were the keenest of foxhunters and only left Warwickshire to make careers in their West Riding family textile firm. Bill was not tall and lifted me about almost acrobatically.

The cost of our various calamities, combined with the economic depression, took their toll on our family finances and in the 1930s these were sadly ailing. It had been decided that, owing to our straitened circumstances, Jimmy could not go to a university, until the Eton authorities pointed out that this would be a waste of good material – so he went to Oxford on a financial shoestring. My father gave up farming as the acreage he rented was too small to be economical. His other sacrifices were to replace the Baby Austin with a bicycle for several months and to give up his minor attempts to defeat the bookies. As Secretary of the Bramham Moor Hunt he was kept busy settling poultry claims with irate farmers and their wives and getting fences repaired after hunting days. Our household was cut to a minimum, which left a lot of work for my mother, who was now deprived of Maurice and others who had shared the extra burden I represented. Just how stark my situation was emerged while I was watching two casual labourers repair a building in the garden. They said it was lucky I was not their daughter because they could not afford to keep me, either in time or money. I knew we suffered from a shortage of funds yet never before had the effects been directly related to my difficulties.

My mother always took us as children to visit patients at the Marguerite Home for Crippled Children which was only a quarter of a mile away. We thought them wonderfully cheerful on their horrible splints but somehow felt they were of a different species. Now it was different. I began to feel we had a lot in common and, as I had my electric chair, I thought they might like me to go and try to read them a good story in serial form. I failed to prepare the ground and had to compete in the ward with the noise of dinners and a volley of backchat amongst the children. On my second visit I decided the backchat was barracking and the bird for me, so regretfully I retired feeling foolish though happy to comply with popular demand.

Concerned about my future, my mother followed the instructions of Sir Robert Jones and travelled to London to consult the Central Council for the Care of Cripples about my education. It proved to be a wasted journey for they had nothing whatever to suggest. A friend proposed that I might be interested in a course in current affairs and public speaking run by the Yorkshire Conservative Office in Leeds. The tutor was partly blind but very astute and the idea was a godsend. Mr Larcom gave his lessons in a ground floor room in Leeds, which tied in well with my physio. sessions. I took great trouble in preparing my speaking lessons and he made me deliver my practice speeches in stentorian tones as if to fill the Albert Hall. He suggested I enter for a public speaking competition which was very exciting because the whole exercise not only revived my interest in politics but was something at which I could compete on level terms with able-bodied people. I was chairman of the team and we came second.

My mother was bombarded by 'helpful' letters and one now recommended an osteopath in London. His name was West and he lived in Hertford Street. Despite the financial implications, my parents decided we must try this for a month. In London, kind people planned to take us to the theatre and only later discovered the difficulty of cajoling a chair up the winding steps and round narrow corners to our places. At everybody's cost I saw three plays, including *Flies In The Sun* with Ivor Novello, Dorothy Dickson and her beautiful daughter, Dorothy Hyson, making her stage début. The theatre was magical and left me no time to think about the harsher aspects of my visit, which were all too evident outside where kerbs were impossible to negotiate. My mother was forced to push me in the wheelchair along the street, dicing with death as she dodged the traffic in Piccadilly Circus.

At least West managed to make me more supple, so our London visit was rated a success. However, the full weight of dealing with me while we were there fell on my mother and, as a result of the terrific strain, she developed a severe attack of eczema. The fact that her presence was indispensible was starkly illustrated one afternoon when she went for treatment and left me to play backgammon with a teenage boy we knew. Suddenly I needed desperately to go to the loo but had no hope of doing so until her return. As neither my father nor the boy could lift me, it would have been pointless to acquaint them with my problem. That impasse was unforgettable and I cannot think how we came through without any sort of mess or muddle.

When we returned to Yorkshire Joan announced her engagement to Tony Yates and we all became involved in compiling lists of guests and of the marvellous presents that rolled in. The Yates brothers and Uncle Hugo introduced Pooh and me to the game of Bridge. I loved to try and play though my fingers and hands were upsettingly unreliable and at any time might fall on the table and sweep everything to the ground. Eventually, it became possible to play cards from my own hand but not from dummy, and I could not deal, but people were long-suffering about my struggling attempts to compete. It was not such a good idea to try me at a village whist drive; while I had often played there and enjoyed it before I was ill, now the 'all change' method meant that I disrupted the whole affair each time, needing experienced help to get me to my feet to change tables.

It had, however, become possible for one expert person to get me on to the loo and out of the bath. For the loo, although I could cope with the paper, I was unable to pull up my pants or sit down or get up without good, strong assistance and in getting me upright it was imperative to stop my feet from slipping. For the bath, Monna's persistence in exercising my left leg enabled me – if supported by someone else – to walk without a splint and sit on the end of the bath into which my legs would be swung and I would be lowered. To get out again I was hauled onto the edge and my legs were swung over before I was stood up and transferred to another chair for drying. It made a tremendous difference to me no longer to feel tied to invalid equipment.

When Joan and Tony went to live a few miles away from us, Bill spent a lot of time in our house. He admired enormously the way my mother was coping with me and became the best person at moving me about. A lifting team consisting of him, my mother and Fred could storm the bastions of the most inaccessible buildings. He certainly increased my mobility a great deal by getting me in and out of the car singlehanded and this led to my going all over the place with him, including to good positions of vantage from which to watch his frequent rides in point-to-point races. While Bill was somewhat erratic and unpredictable, in most situations he had the most sympathetic heart and was hilariously entertaining, lively and original. It was through no fault of his that I formed for him an inconvenient and unrequited passion, a situation which had still more complications. While I suffered these agonised teenage pangs the object of my affections was busily plighting his secret and unsuccessful troth to Prudence. Mentally, I committed every kind of loathsome crime to deter that romance, especially as it was mainly conducted in the cellar where the store was for the tea Pooh kept for the agency with which she still persevered. Partly in order to reduce my mother's workload, Bill swept me off with a helper to stay for a week-end with a mutual friend of his and my family's who lived in Leicestershire. It was thrilling to make this first venture forth independent of the family, and it went extremely well. Next, Bill suggested that he and Pooh should take me to his home at Broughton Grange, near Banbury, to stay with his parents. Again all went very well.

Now that my mother could travel with me alone, she drove me several times to London to see new doctors and quacks whose names had been forced upon her. There was 'Jock the Cobbler', strongly recommended for fixing shoes in a magic way. He lived in the suburbs and his waiting-room was full of all sorts and shapes of clients. It occurred to me early on that while he might be excellent for corns and bunions, even for legs and feet, to be faced with all of me must be more than he could manage. It did not take him long to say that mine really was a more extensive case than he was used to; nevertheless, he was prepared to do his best for me with a pair of shoes. I handed these over with great reluctance because of our constant difficulty in obtaining suitable footwear, so it was a relief when they came back little harmed if not at all improved.

Undoubtedly, the most helpful of these strange pick-ups was

Pat Leahy. Having lost a leg in the 1914–18 war he had found in hospital that he could help both himself and other patients by exercising 'mind over matter'. He now practised in Clarges Street and as he had rescued Bill Yates from the throes of a nervous breakdown he started on a good wicket with me. There was no doubt that he had a salubrious, if hypnotic, influence. At the end of our interview he wrote for me a post card which read: 'Confidence and comfort will increase each day and with it power. Your left hand will lift if you now close your eyes.' As I type this it is all I can do to keep my left hand on the keyboard and to this day if I repeat those words there is a noticeable effect both on my muscles and my outlook. With hindsight I greatly regret that I did not direct his attention to my *right* hand which utterly refuses to lift itself unaided!

Visits to Pat Leahy were nothing if not encouraging and treatment with Monna was never depressing because it was both constructive and realistic. On the other hand this was not the case with the other so-called 'cures'. There were quacks who either gave me the creeps or were so earnest in their approach that I wanted to burst into bitter tears of impotence on the spot. I wanted to know what right they had to come in at this late stage and emphasise my crippled state without knowing the stress and strain we had been through to get this far. What right had they to wag their heads and look gloomy now? My heart sank every time a new such name cropped up for I did not feel they were competent to deal with my total situation. Maybe they were used to one limb or even two which needed treatment, but when everything was affected they could not cope. By now I had begun to get myself together with the help of my mother and the family, enough to live life with a lighter heart, but these 'weirdies' could be relied on to render my spirits heavy as lead.

Getting suitable clothes for me became less of a problem now that I could be stood up to try things on, but finding footwear was horrendous. While the splintmakers had to supply the hideous full-length caliper splint, (a piece of apparatus that was invaluable in holding my knee and leg rigid and giving me confidence to stand firmly) their shoes and boots were extremely ugly and uncomfortable and I would do almost anything to avoid them. My feet were very long and narrow, but because of bad circulation my left foot became swollen and needed pliable covering, yet the caliper fitting called for the harshest leather. It consisted of clumsy metal holes set into the heels of the shoe and held together by a metal bar under the sole. By sheer good luck we discovered in the Leeds Lotus shop someone who became touchingly interested in our boring problem. He knew about the light aluminium material for aircraft and soon used it to make a much neater set of caliper fittings for me. With these I could then get sleeker and more comfortable shoes which also turned out to be a lot cheaper than the horrible surgical variety.

It was also difficult to find a suitable tray or table for me to use for reading, writing and eating. My hands tried to play halma, draughts and backgammon and for these contests we set up a games board on my knee. On this principle we arranged for a permanent board to lie across my knees, thereby extending the mobility potential of my hand and lower arm. If the board went for six it scattered its load far and wide and I then had to yell furiously for helpers who came, at great inconvenience, from all corners of the house. My writing was still very wobbly, developed on the lines of pushing my right hand along on my wristbone without lifting up the arm, which is the technique I still use today.

After a two year interval we planned a return trip to Bembridge. By sending my electric chair ahead of us by rail and with my much safer standing and dogged attempts at hobbling along, this visit was a less immobile affair for me. On the way down we stopped for lunch with a friend of Jimmy's called Anne Loyd, whom he subsequently married. She lived at Lockinge, an enormous Victorian house near Wantage which was only two miles off our route and conveniently had no front door step. We found the Loyds an enchanting family. There were two sons and three daughters, a third son having recently died at school of this wretched polio. They were all extremely kind and understanding about our difficulties and we enjoyed our visit so much that we only just caught the ferry to the Isle of Wight.

The Solent was full of the Royal Navy for the Silver Jubilee Spithead Review and some kind enthusiasts thought it would be nice for me to go in a boat to have a look at the men of war. It had been found possible to carry me in what is known as a 'chair lift', requiring two stalwarts to link hands under my seat and again above my waist before we took off. Employing this method I was lowered into a motor boat by carriers knee deep in seawater because the tide was in. We chugged out merrily with a suitably Jubilee sun pouring down from the heavens. There was great excitement when we came within nodding distance of the warships, which was also close enough to see the leftovers and cabbage leaves from their lunch. Jubilation satisfied, we chugged for home. All of a sudden there were unwilling noises from our engine, and then no noises at all.

We bobbed about mid-ocean under the glaring sun until, after an hour and a half of determined efforts to get the obstinate engine going, we made a concerted attempt to attract attention to our plight. Fortunately, we had a glamorous young lady with us and she managed to catch the eye of the Admiral's pinnace which then proceeded to tow us home in great style. The tide was now out and we had to land on a treacherously slippery long stretch of rocky causeway covered in shells and seaweed with deep sea on either side. The only means of getting me ashore was to carry me over this death-trap. I shall never know how my carriers – my mother and Oliver Stobart – kept their footing, especially as they had to carry me sideways to fit on to the causeway. If one of them had slipped we must all have been injured and quite probably drowned.

The 16th/ 5th Lancers came to be quartered at York and, after a year or so, Pooh became engaged to Captain R.V. Taylor, Bob, who already knew Jimmy from Oxford days. He shared our interests and they both very kindly included me in their parties; by now I was old enough to notice that some people were co-ordinated and welcoming and treated me like anybody else, while others soon decided there was nothing going for them with me and veered off elsewhere. With the first I had the advantage of their natural wish to help, but the others were embarrassed and knotted up, if not plain bored, by my cumbersome appearance. I was happy about Pooh and Bob and never felt a twinge of envy or fear of loneliness; in this I was helped by neighbours who gathered me up and provided interesting distractions.

My aunt discovered it was possible to go on a three week Mediterranean cruise for £50, so my parents decided to take me. Because it was so cheap we knew we were taking pot luck and could stipulate no special requirements for me, but we were accompanied by Aunt Esmée, Simon and a girl friend who was an attractive and aspiring young actress. The Brooksbank chair came too. Of these companions only Simon could help my mother to carry me, for my father was ruled out by arthritis and the others could hardly lift a flea. Directly we boarded *Atlantis* we observed a number of hefty obstacles, such as a bunk to be climbed into, and difficult loos and baths. At that point my mother's spirits, like my own, sank to zero. There were those humps on the floor to get over in the chair and Simon found that the best way to tackle this was at the run with the chair tipped on its back wheels; when we first barged into the dining-room in this manner with my legs in the air, we greatly surprised our fellow passengers. After a few days they got used to us, and in return we took care to try not to impede their progress or activities.

The 'Cook's homme' became our firm ally and got me into every port of call. For Ceuta, I was held on a donkey. For Athens, I was carried by two burly tars down the ship's perpendicular ladder and deposited in a boat below. Our day there was superb and marked one of my mother's most notable achievements – when she carried me on a kitchen chair, with the help of a Greek guide, to the very top of the Acropolis. On the way up we passed several *Atlantis* passengers wilting by the wayside from the effort of their own climb. When we wished to return to the ship in the evening a storm had blown up and was lashing the sea into a frenzy. A sailor carried me over his shoulder in a 'fireman's lift', and, as the boat washed upwards, he jumped with his burden onto the landing-stage where the ship's engineer just managed to catch us and push us up the perpendicular ladder. We had made it, but when the next boatload sought to embark the ladder was swept off the side of the ship.

At Constantinople we viewed Santa Sofia and the Blue Mosque and were then urged to visit a mosque with especially beautiful mosaics. This meant climbing steps so I stayed in the hired car. The others had just disappeared out of view when the driver turned round with a broad grin and gabbled something unintelligible. Starting the car he drove off at high speed, laughing cheerfully as I bumped about in the back. We raced down bumpy, cobbled streets and I longed to get to the window to scream out. I had visions of wild hills and dark forests and when at last we passed outside the city gates, these very hills and forests loomed up over the driver's cap. I thought: 'This is it. Now I shall never be heard of again.' Suddenly the car swung round in a great lurch and the driver, with a beaming face, waved his arms to direct my eye to a wonderful mass of cherry blossom cascading over the city walls. Now I saw that he had brought me to see this to make up for missing the mosaics. The drive back seemed no distance and the others returned to find me sitting just where they had left me. It was hard to persuade them to believe my story.

In Malta, we visited the Hall of the Knights Templar and I unwisely chose to practise my walking exercises on the free floorspace offered, conscious that my exercises had been neglected on the unsteady shipboard. The floor of the Hall is constructed of fine marble and, after only a few steps, my feet shot from under me and I dragged my mother down with me as we landed in a crashing fall. If there had been a handy X-ray machine I thought it must surely have found cracks and splinterings in both of us, but luckily the huge bruises disappeared eventually with no lasting effects. We spent a good day at Lisbon, visiting the gardens at Cintra and the casino at Estoril.

When we returned, Jimmy announced that he was going to marry Anne Loyd, having already enjoyed a long unofficial engagement. We already thought of her as a member of the family and both she and her parents had been very kind about my problems. Anne's brother, John, had just joined the Coldstream Guards; her sister, Hester, was fourteen and doing lessons at home, while the twins, Christopher and Catherine, were eleven. Hester quickly became a friend of mine and, even though she was nearly three years younger, proved a fascinating companion in any situation. She had a very generous heart and a penetrating sense of humour, together with a fertile imagination. Going to stay there meant endless fun and interest, and with my improved walking I could quite well tackle the long distances inside Lockinge. Our only trouble was the stairs, but someone always helped my mother to give me a chair lift up and down each day.

The Loyds asked my parents whether they would like to take me to stay with them for Ascot Races. We thought out carefully whether we could manage to get me about there without being an embarrassment to all and sundry. Once we had worked things out we accepted with delight, though we did have misgivings on the first day during our mammoth walk to the enclosure from our picnic lunch in the car park. Our plan had been to get me there and deposit me on a seat, but we kept meeting friends of my mother's who did not realise the precarious state we were in. When at last we reached the steps where we had to adopt our stair-climbing routine, my right foot turned firmly downwards doing its very best to trip us up. We only just made it. Next day the car dropped us much nearer the paddock, so we had no trouble. Already I had become fond of racing at Wetherby and York, having discovered that in the camaraderie and shared interest of racing the usual barrier of disability disappeared. Given a good point of vantage, a form book and a few firm friends and runners, I found that here was an activity to be entered into on level terms.

When Gavin Fairfax wrote to tell us about a spiritual healer, my hackles rose. However, Gavin's success with the electric chair gave me great respect for his advice and, once I was assured that this man would not be another Hickson, I soon agreed to go and see him. This time Jimmy was to be the lamb to the slaughter and I accompanied him to an address in a north London square. The man seemed pleasant, if innocuous, but he took an instant dislike to my lipstick and nail varnish which he declared was proof that the spirit was all wrong. How, he asked, did I expect to get better if I was determined to blot out the spirit with this camouflage? He said this stood to reason because the spirit fed the nerves and the nerves fed the muscles so there was no wonder that my muscles did not work. I peered at Jimmy and felt highly relieved to note a puzzled twinkle in his eye. We heard the fellow out in silence, both feeling he was a trifle nuts. It was good to have Jimmy as witness that I could become a sitting target for well-meaning people who wished to dominate their victims with strange theories. We took a taxi home.

My mother and I had worked out a satisfactory method for taxis. I stood propped against the open door while she went round and got inside, put down the little seat and prepared to haul me on to it by the shoulders, if possible assisted by the taxi driver who was asked to push and lift me by the knees. Once on the seat it was simple to be swivelled round and then, unless on a very perilous journey, I could keep my balance quite well. To dismount was less complicated but more painful, as the dead weight of my legs scraped on the sharp edge of the running-board and often skinned the back of my legs in the process. Nevertheless, as I could not use either tubes or buses it was invaluable to have this means of transport in London, so I kept quiet about this snag.

My mother received yet another well intentioned letter recommending a doctor, this time in Lausanne. Once again the faithful Simon and Aunt Esmée accompanied us, which not only helped us financially but also increased our opportunity for mirth.

We had worked out a routine for loading and unloading me on English trains, but French trains proved more difficult. Our usual method was to enlist the help of two porters who would lift me off the platform and hand me to my mother who would be standing in the doorway, from which point we shuffled along together and sat me down in the carriage. French trains ride very high off the platform but Simon proved a veritable tower of strength in getting me on board. Having overslept, we reached Lausanne with only eight minutes for my mother to dress herself and me. Only our pillows went on to Turin.

Directly on arrival we presented ourselves at the doctor's clinic. He announced that I should attend his gymnasium daily and work on half a dozen different exercise machines. He explained that this was more than he would usually prescribe but he did so now because with me there was such general loss of musclepower. He could say that again! He said that if he appeared distracted – which he did not – it was due to the arrival of his first grandchild the night before. We went to the gymnasium the next day and queued for one hour to use the first machine; to get on to the rest involved similar delays. Throughout this long and tedious day Simon and my mother assisted other patients to clamber on and off their prescribed machines. The only two staff on duty were desperately overworked and in their hurried handling reduced the back of my left leg to a hideously raw area which became delicate and sore and in need of attention for many weeks. We stayed in Lausanne for a month, hoping the doctor might reappear with words of wisdom which might indicate it was worth leaving me there for some months but he never did. We went on hired trips round the Lake, to Gstaad and the Chateau de Chillon. Monna dashed over to see if she could find anything new there to help me. Finally, we all decided to return to England. Before leaving, my mother sent a tart note to the doctor, from whom she received an equally tart reply. We felt we had been sold short and returned to London in a sombre mood, so it was especially soothing to be taken out to dinner on arrival by Mr Loyd. Jimmy and Anne had been married at Lockinge that winter.

Two young men who came into our lives separately during the 1930s and have remained our great friends ever since are Brian Johnston and Martin Gilliat. Brian, broadcaster and cricket commentator, appeared shy and retiring when Jimmy brought him to stay with us while they were both at Oxford, but by the end of his visit we knew this to be an absurd illusion. The days he was with us were riotous and he delighted me by shrewdly making fun of my immobility. He is now happily married with a family of five and I am godmother to his elder daughter. Martin Gilliat was brought to us by the Stobarts, a tall young man with ginger hair and an amazingly quick wit who could lighten the most difficult situation. It is not surprising that, as Lt Col Sir Martin Gilliat, KCVO, MBE, he has been private secretary to HM Queen Elizabeth the Queen Mother for many years. Still unmarried, Martin has enough lady friends to keep everyone guessing but always finds time for us. I mention these two men because, despite their important careers, both have kept all their magical qualities. Prudence and Bob had a wonderful wedding from Walton and we were delighted to have our two Filey fishermen, Jenks and Cammish, resplendent with huge buttonholes, amongst the gathering of friends and relations. A few months later the bridal pair left with the regiment for India. This was a bit traumatic, especially as it coincided with the moment when Mr Larcom moved away from Leeds and ended my classes. Worse still, the incomparable Monna got married and moved to North

Yorkshire. I grew gloomy and was constantly assailed by dismal thoughts of what might become of me. Walton House was now too big for us so my mother courageously took her problem to a generous childhood friend and to Uncle Hugo Stobart, and was thus provided with funds to build a house. It was planned with ground-floor bedroom and bathroom accommodation for me and was a way of openly accepting that it was now unlikely that I should ever get much better. The Bramham Park Estate kindly allowed my parents to choose a site on which to build. They selected one three fields away from our old house, on a hilltop, with panoramic views.

While the building progressed I and a helper stayed at Lockinge where John and Hester gave me a marvellous time. They got me about all over the place and one day I even hobbled with them half a mile down St Giles in Oxford because there seemed to be no other way to reach the car. When Hester 'came out' the following summer, I stayed with her in London for three weeks. Friends took us to dinner or to the theatre and I used to pinch myself to think this was really me, independent of family and flitting around merrily. It often occurred to me that it was extremely unusual for someone so pretty and in demand to have the time to drag around with her such a clumsy appendage, but Hester had unique qualities. Her apt commentary certainly inspired interest and happiness. When I was with her I readily dismissed all worries about the future.

At the theatre one evening I was tapped on the shoulder by a Colonel Blimp when I failed to stand up for the National Anthem. He said I should be ashamed of myself. His ranting stopped abruptly as two of our party hauled me to my feet, whereupon he became full of obsequious apology and acute embarrassment – poor chap.

For some months Simon worked in Kenya on his father's farm and then returned to start a course at the Cirencester Agricultural College. This was within reach of Lockings so Hester and I went there to watch him play the lead in a theatrical production. Afterwards, they carried me up miles of stone stairs to his room, at which point Simon remembered that students were banned from entertaining females in their rooms. I had ugly visions of this causing his dismissal so we raced downstairs while the authorities fortunately remained blind and deaf to us.

Simon informed me that he intended to settle in Kenya and asked if I would go there with him to keep house, whether or not he decided to marry anyone. He knew that I should make a rotten housekeeper and I am convinced that his plan was to save my mother from worrying about my future. He stuck to his suggestion even when I drew his attention to its worst aspects, so I was both flattered and grateful. We decided not to tell anyone about the proposition just yet. It was exhilarating to be included like this, for to be disabled and see friends of the same age making plans and careers, is upsetting. To be unable to move your arms not only prevents you from undertaking many everyday activities but also cuts you off from ordinary social intercourse – you often cannot shake hands nor hold hands without a lot of arrangement, and you can never hold out your arms to throw them round someone in an embrace. Opportunities for sexual activity are reduced accordingly.

In the summer of 1939 the Yorkshire Association for the Care of Cripples appointed me their Appeals Organiser. I had been trying frantically to think of some possible occupation and so welcomed the idea. It was suggested that I should approach a number of eminent Yorkshire people to ask for their financial support for a scheme to raise the standard of the almost non-existent care service for the disabled in the county, and to work towards an inaugural meeting in the autumn. As my activities would take me all over the county, I could employ someone at thirty shillings a week to drive me round and act as secretary, but I would receive no remuneration myself on the grounds that it might prove difficult to 'tout' for funds if I were paid. By now I could type reasonably with one finger, and my helper and I got a remarkably good response to our appeals by letter, in person and through public meetings.

The building of Mill Hill House was now complete. It was an E-shaped house, in stone with red pantile roof. The porch and front door were in the middle, one end contained my ground floor bed-sittingroom and bathroom with a spare room and bathroom above. The middle contained a fair-sized drawing-room, small dining-room, smoking-room and pantry, with the main bedrooms on top. The far wing had the kitchen and a maisonette where Fred Shutt and his wife and daughter lived. To approach the house entailed a stern climb up from the road, but once you got to the top of the hill the view was surprisingly open and rural. Most of our best furniture could be fitted in and the house was particularly light and cheerful. It covered a much smaller area than Walton House and the work involved in maintaining it was considerably less. There were two drawbacks from my point of view: the steep drive often proved too much for my electric chair and was impassable in the snow, and while the parquet floors saved carpets, they were very treacherous for walking on in a caliper splint.

Hester was staying with us at Mill Hill in August 1939 when plans for the Government Evacuation Scheme were announced, so we quickly put her on the train for Lockinge. This was the end of my fairytale era. Simon was already doing his national service when war was declared, so, for him, the news made little difference. Jimmy joined the Grenadier Guards, and as Pooh was home with us for leave after two years in India she now waited for Bob to return with his regiment to set up house in England. It was lovely to have her at home, despite the gathering gloom.

4

Wartime

In September 1939 no fewer than 1,900 evacuees were dumped into the Wetherby reception area and, as WVS evacuation officer for the Rural District, my mother had to billet them and face the consequences. She had headquarters in the Council Offices and unending problems to solve. Thinking I might be dive-bombed if left at home on my own, she took me with her, and although there were sharp steps to tackle these did not prove insuperable.

The Yorkshire Association's plans for an inaugural meeting in the autumn were cancelled so now I badly needed occupation and was delighted to be asked to help the Council staff by checking off the billeting forms. After a few days on this job we were visited by a Ministry of Health Inspector who coolly said that as they needed to employ a billeting clerk he wondered if I would take the job for thirty shillings a week? He could not possibly have known that this was to be one of the most thrilling moments of my life. To be provided with this unexpected side-door into paid employment was invaluable. Now I clocked in each morning at 9.30 a.m. and was there until 5.30 p.m. Before long I was appointed Acting Chief Billeting Officer with a significant increase in pay.

Billeting crises and excitements abounded. One day a panic call came from an outlying village to say that a mother was planning to abscond, taking one child with her and leaving three in the billet. My mother rushed over to find the mother gone, having thumbed a lift on a removal van. A chase followed and the van was caught, after which the family was happily re-united and re-billeted. My mother and the Clerk to the Council had to hide behind the post office counter to catch one very sophisticated mother who conned a naive householder into keeping her child while she walked the streets of Leeds, then forged the householder's name on the billeting form and kept the money. They caught her redhanded actually drawing the cash and although the Ministry refused to bring any case, fright stopped the lady from doing this again.

I used to sit all day on a hard office chair but the table was at just the right height so I had no aches or pains. The day was full and busy. It soon became imperative to set up a hostel for 'unbilletables' and my mother prepared a suitable house. What was missing was the right warden. When the inmates had intimidated all the existing helpers, we advertised for more. The only response came from a lady aged sixty-five, Miss Rae, retired after long service with blind babies and now wanting to do war work. I was asked to interview her and fell completely for her white hair, pink and white complexion and blue eyes, so it was with great reluctance that I decided she was unsuitable for our tough job and said so. Immediately she asked for details of these villainous children and I painted as dark a picture as possible. Nothing put her off and she soon asked when she might start work. Knowing there were no other applicants it was really Hobson's choice, but it felt like throwing an early Christian martyr to the hungry lions.

Peace reigned at the hostel within one week of Miss Rae's arrival. She got control of those really dangerous hooligans and they soon vied with each other to sing in the church choir which was how she rewarded good behaviour. In Miss Rae's view nobody deserved to have a bad name and her discipline was based on love and vigilance. Her charges fell under the spell and she quickly transformed the hostel into a cosy family home with the inmates helping throughout, so it was hard to believe that only two weeks earlier the police had been called there to protect the staff from gang warfare. The Ministry of Health was dazzled by this transformation and made the hostel a show piece for staff from far and wide. Miss Rae cured petty pilferers, thugs, and inveterate bed-wetters in the name of God and Winston Churchill. She was still there on VE Day and at some stage received the MBE.

Beneficent though the Government Evacuation scheme often proved to be, it was not without its cruel aspects, and not only for the householders. For instance, on arrival the 'unaccompanied schoolchildren' were all grouped together in a school yard for the locals to make their selections. Some were left to the last and in this way we got Charles, Arnold and Donald. Nobody had chosen these three ragged, grimy little boys who came from the seamiest of Leeds backgrounds. Their drunken, belligerent old father had a wife who had wisely disappeared and when his sons were billeted with us his one aim was to come out and frighten 'the lady', but in that he had not bargained for my mother. The boys were delighted when he left; he did not come again. By the time they were bathed, tidily dressed and well fed, they started to enjoy life at Walton, except that they kept talking about their sister Gladys.

Gladys was still in Leeds because she was under five and had no mother to accompany her as an evacuee. A kindly householder in Wetherby agreed to house her, and when my mother went to the house in Leeds she found there a little golden-haired girl asleep under a heap of filthy rags in a front room littered with tins and garbage. She delightedly took my mother's hand and accompanied her to the country. Her father was told of her whereabouts by the education authority and he then steered clear.

The children adapted quickly to civilized living habits, contributing their own shrewd observations on the way.

'Ain't Mr Fox lucky?' said Donald. When asked why, he replied, 'Well, Mr Shutt cleans 'is boots and Mrs Fox makes 'is bed.' Boots and beds were two of the least favourite jobs in their family.

Then, after a look round at the reasonable contents of our house, Stanley asked: 'Did Mr Fox win a lottery, Miss?' My father and I played halma with them and he impressed on them that cheating really did not pay.

My mother, however, decided that I must have a lunchtime break from the office and this required *us* to cheat a bit, over petrol. She was not thinking about food but about the loo, because at the Council Offices there were more steps down to get there than I could tackle, so she was determined that for the good of my bladder I must go home mid day. Before long I convinced her that my accommodating inside could hold on until after five, so the lunchtime journey ceased.

My father looked out of his window one day and spotted men digging deep holes two fields away. They seemed persistent and their researches resulted in the erection of the Royal Ordnance Factory, designed to employ 16,000 workers, situated on the area overlooked by the south-facing windows of our new house. The horrific plan was to manufacture high explosives. Mill Hill House now became a sitting target. While good friends advised us to move the house value slumped dramatically; which reinforced our decision to stay put.

Suddenly and unexpectedly, my sister Joan died in February 1940. This was an appalling shock for all of us, particularly her husband. My parents had been especially devoted to their gifted firstborn child whose dynamic attraction won her admirers at every level, and, selfishly perhaps, I knew I had lost a stalwart helper who supplied both the encouragement and the provocation I sorely needed. Struck dumb by a sense of loss, I felt somehow that she had been let down. She had deeply loved her son Timothy with whom she was very close, and when my mother explained to him that she would not be coming back he was both brave and trusting. Our tightly-knit family found it hard to bear this tragedy.

Shortly afterwards Pooh and Bob announced they were to have a baby, so Nannie Holland went there after leaving Timothy, for whom a governess was engaged by his father. After Dunkirk for several days we had no news of Jimmy, but at last he turned up. He had lived through some dangerous escapades in France where he had been potted in the leg by a sniper, then rescued from The Channel by a padré and was now safely in hospital in Kent. We were thankful to hear from Martin Gilliat's mother that Martin was a prisoner of war after the ghastly battle of Calais. For the next five years I wrote him boring screeds, his replies to which never contained a disconsolate note, instead providing bright spots in the weeks, months and years until the war ended.

Simon, now a 2nd Lieutenant in the Coldstream Guards, came to Mill Hill House on the news that he was going overseas. It was a tame, rather pointless meeting, where none of us had the heart to say anything worthwhile. It was not long before I started to get his letters from the desert; one contained a perspex ring which he claimed was part of a Messerschmidt's windscreen.

I buried myself in the considerable amount of work to be done at the office. The other Council Office employees became firm friends. There was one-legged Tim on the telephones; six-foot Mr Harvey, who was said to have nearly died when he stretched up to open a window and burst an ulcer; Olive, who declared that certain other members of staff 'got a bit funny' with her in the strong room, though she never failed to don a seductive velveteen for all Council meetings. Harold Smith, the Clerk of the Council, was extremely understanding of my problems. He had his own disability of a slight spinal curvature and one leg being shorter than the other which he never alluded to but which may have helped me! The atmosphere was good and I welcomed the request to undertake for them the billeting of war workers for the Ordnance Factory. I had met already the Factory's dynamic superintendent who was to achieve astonishing results from 16,000 wartime employees, most of whom were little more than 'odds and sods'. The Council now conducted a survey which revealed a number of households prepared to take in wartime lodgers.

Our family finances again began to give trouble and the final wrench came when we had to part with Fred and Margaret Shutt. With admirable resilience Fred got a job with better pay as a mechanic at the munitions factory, so he and his family moved into a council house in Walton. My mother told me she intended to become a wage-earner, if possible at the Factory where there appeared to be money to burn. The trouble was that as she had no recognised qualifications she must aim to get a humble, boring job. This made me choke with rage and guilt, knowing that she could have been highly qualified but for me. Thinking furiously, I suddenly saw that the answer might be in my own hands. The head of the labour department was calling at my office the next week in search of living accommodation.

When he arrived, I assured him that I had a number of likely addresses of attractive flats, but added that before I gave him them, my mother wanted a job in his department. Heaven knows how I was so brazen, but these tactics got her the coveted interview and she was duly appointed Labour Officer with special responsibilities for staff hostels and canteens. She worked hard and with great dash until the war ended, when she earned high commendation.

Under these changed conditions I employed a series of ladies to dress and undress me, bath me, drive me to the office or elsewhere, and take me by train to London when I had leave. Because of my job, combined with my immobility, looking after me ranked as a reserved occupation. The family car was continually requisitioned for my use, so my mother had either to use a bicycle or my father's precious Baby Austin. My father had adjusted to his new rôle with no fuss and now took responsibility for the stoking, the hens, a lot of washing up and the garden. On Wednesdays he took the bus to Wetherby to queue for our weekly cake from a lady confectioner called Turvey, whom he privately christened 'Topsy'.

Much as I liked my work it would not qualify me for post-war employment and I was told that a diploma in social work from Leeds University would be both useful and relevant. In order to discover whether the authorities at Leeds University would be ready to take on someone with my extent of physical disability, I went there to be interviewed. The panel was composed of three men and a woman. At the sight of me their eyes filled with tears and they shook their heads forlornly. They then pulled themselves together and were nothing if not hardboiled in telling me that they could not even consider my application owing to my severe physical handicaps, on account of the many steps in the university and the black-out. I half hoped they might have had an alternative suggestion, but they had none.

Because she was working, my mother did not come to that interview but she sensed my disappointment, so she at once collaborated with me on a response to an advertisement that caught my eye in *The Times*. It told of London University's waiving the normal entrance exam for severely disabled people. We quickly applied for an interview and planned that after the snub received from Leeds, we would play down my disability as far as possible.

When we got to the university we discovered that the waiting-room was next to the interviewing room and this enabled my mother to straighten my caliper pull me to my feet and, with unseen hands, push me round the door. I could only stand propped against the wall, but from that position I seemed to get on quite well with the questions. Afterwards, I hobbled back to Mamma and we congratulated ourselves that I had not disclosed that if I sat down I could not get up without a lot of help. In the train my mother told me she would try to evolve some method of tackling my living arrangements during the course and we returned home feeling mildly jubilant and full of plans. Three weeks later a letter arrived to tell me that I was not disabled enough to qualify for the University's special course! I am not quite certain why I did not come clean then and write to explain our deception. I now suspect the real truth was that I simply had not the heart to do so.

When the post of secretary to the Marguerite Hepton Memorial Orthopaedic Hospital – the old Marguerite Home for Crippled Children – was advertised, I applied. My mother was chairman of the hospital but was not on the selection committee which, in the circumstances, was just as well. The former secretary had joined the forces and I was one of four applicants. I was not at all surprised to be turned down in favour of a highly qualified applicant from Guy's Hospital who was also slightly disabled, but three days after he took up the post he found the work did not suit him and walked out. The committee then looked for the applicant who lived nearest, so the job was offered to me. The RDC released me and the Clerk of the Council bothered to come to the Hospital to show me the accountancy system, knowing I was determined to prove the job was within my capacity, never mind the twisting flight of slippery stairs which two people had to carry me up and down each day. There were ninety in-patients, mostly admitted for periods of one to six years with only one day a week for visiting. On the pay-roll were a semi-resident doctor, two physiotherapists, a nursing staff of thirty-five or so, three school teachers, cooks and domestic workers and two gardeners. With weekly and monthly wage packets to calculate, catering and establishment accounts to keep, ration cards and pay-as-you-earn tax returns to settle, there was no shortage of occupation. I drove to the office each day in my electric chair.

After a few months a groundfloor office was contrived for me out of a corner of a ward. The general office was next door and housed an indispensable clerk typist. It was up to me to take the Committee minutes and to carry out the subsequent negotiations with local authorities and hospital organisations. The Matron was a great ally, though her orders could be a bit peremptory, and the unfortunate maintenance engineer was told once to 'Catch all mice!' Organising the flag day for the Leeds Invalid Children's Aid Society was part of my remit, since the proceeds were devoted to the hospital. I scoured Leeds to discover ways to get collecting-tins into schools and factories but the effort was rewarded when the total sum raised increased from £400 to £1,100. These funds were much needed because payments from local authorities for their patients did not cover rising prices, and items like bed tables, sun-blinds, drive repairs and outside painting always depended on voluntary provision. Quite unexpectedly, funds began to roll in from a different source – workers at the Royal Ordnance Factory who saw child patients across the road suddenly decided to raise £1,000 to help the hospital.

I was lucky enough to have a friendly neighbour who offered me voluntary and meticulous help. He was recovering from a serious illness and so was rendered unfit for national service, but he was very good-looking and drove a Jaguar car, so from the first time he came to give me his loyal and splendid support my stock rose amongst the nursing staff.

I lunched daily at the hospital and in the break had treatment from the physiotherapists who submerged my legs and feet in deep baths with electrodes to get rid of those dreaded chilblains. We saw no immediate results, but six years later the chilblains vanished, though I cannot be certain whether this was due to the after-effects of this sustained treatment or not.

One of the happiest reunions brought about by my hospital job was with Monna. The hospital was short of two physios, so I got Monna to fill in, which she did with customary aplomb and excellence. She now had a daughter, and a rocky marriage, so again she was hard at work. We picked up where we had left off and she was not displeased with my progress.

The dreaded news arrived that Simon was missing, believed wounded, after the North African Battle of Knightsbridge. There was a period of dreadful waiting. It seemed most likely that he was on a German boat known to have gone down when taking prisoners to Germany. Not one more word was heard of his whereabouts, despite minute and extensive enquiries made by Aunt Esmée. I was determined not to wallow in unproductive sentiment, since my emotions had been so uselessly battered by Joan's dying. I did not need to be reminded of all that Simon had meant and of our shared happiness; he had left to me his funny little collection of crystal ornaments, together with £500.

When Bob's battalion was preparing to go overseas, Prudence brought their daughter, Maria, and Nannie to live in one end of Mill Hill. Maria was a pretty, engaging little girl and Bob delighted in her whenever he got leave. He and Prudence were very happy and he could not have had a more loving family when he went off to North Africa. But a few weeks later a telegram arrived at Mill Hill. Because none of the family was at home it was delivered to me at the hospital. The contents of the odious yellow envelope told us Bob had been killed.

After finishing his job as adjutant at Sandhurst, Jimmy was posted with a lot more soldiery to Gilling in North Yorkshire. Brian Johnston was one of several of our friends who went there. We knew that John Loyd had been badly wounded in the leg in North Africa so were delighted to get a call from him back home at Lockinge. He asked to stay with us en route to visit his batman's family in Middlesbrough. He looked faintly drawn on arrival but was as beloved and happy-making as ever, and had determined plans to take me and my current helper to London to meet Hester. I soon wangled three days' leave. They left me to select a play and, to my constant chagrin, I chose a dud – down many stairs. When I returned to Yorkshire Hester telephoned with the agonising news that John had contracted a very serious respiratory condition. To my horror I remembered that he had carried me up the flights of theatre steps and shuddered to think that this great effort might have precipitated his illness. I consulted the doctor at the hospital and could not believe it when he said that, from the symptoms described, John would probably die within a month. This prognosis proved only too right. John was nursed solely by his sisters, Hester and Catherine, and by his mother, and when he died the whole family was overwhelmed by the deepest sense of loss. All his friends were distraught to lose someone so very special.

Prudence read good reports in a Sunday paper of a German-Jewish refugee, called Berberich, who was working successfully with polio sufferers and other 'cripples'. He lived in Leeds and claimed to have miraculous electric hands, so we went to visit him. By now I did not believe there was any easy cure. However, I knew that anything to alleviate the struggle would be more than welcome. We were impressed by this man's obvious competence and he agreed to come to Walton to treat me three times a week before I left for work. This meant that he left his home at 5.00 a.m., travelled by bus thirteen miles to Wetherby where he changed buses for Walton and walked the last half mile to Mill Hill. He certainly stimulated activity, was always on time and never grumbled or complained. His hair-raising stories of just escaping a concentration camp but of being compelled to leave his wife, son and daughter back in Germany, left me ashamed to be anything but grateful for my comparatively simple life. After six months of treatment things became complicated when Berberich began to attach too much importance to seeing me. I decided to give it a rest, but was glad that other patients were more loyal to him.

Aunt Esmée was heartbroken by Simon's death and constantly worried about her other sons. Having re-married, she now lived in London with her second husband, Ian Fairbairn. She was engrossed in the W.V.S. Tothill Street 'shop', an early form of citizen's advice bureau which helped people shocked and perplexed by wartime conditions, often with homes bombed and families scattered. She seemed as happy as possible when she came to stay with us and was still very beautiful. We looked forward to her next visit.

Jimmy was again wounded, though not seriously, when he and his colleagues were launched into Europe, so we blessed our good luck. Once out of hospital, he and Anne came to stay at Mill Hill. We scraped the bottom of the petrol can and went to the theatre in Leeds. On our return, the telephone was ringing as we opened the front door. My mother answered. It was Ian, to say that Aunt Esmée had just been killed by a flying-bomb in their home in London. This was a real tragedy for she was so much adored by Ian, by her sons and by all of us; my mother and she were the closest of friends. It was a ghastly blow.

Prudence and I were persuaded to go to a cinema in Tadcaster one Saturday afternoon. There we picked up German measles. Just three weeks to the day later we both became smothered in rash and felt so rotten we could not believe this was the right diagnosis. I found it became very hard to breathe for it went straight to a polio weakened lung. Later I developed asthma as a direct result, but the doctor said he could do nothing to help. My sister-in-law saw my frequent breathing struggles and thought of them when she was impatiently queuing at a chemist's counter in London. The man ahead said that he was content to wait, if necessary for hours, for an antibiotic solution to use in the inhaler which relieved his asthma spasms. Anne thought the description of his difficulties sounded much the same as mine so told me of his remedy. It was an instant success and for the next twenty-nine years an inhaler of his type was my constant companion and often my resuscitator.

Hester wrote to tell me of her engagement to Guy Knight, a former brother officer of John's. I had not cried nor carried on through all our sad events so heaven only knows why I now wept for hours. Life is strange, for I had nothing against Guy and when I saw his photograph had to concede that he looked splendid. Perhaps I had subconsciously, and quite unreasonably, relied on Hester to be my means of leading an independent life and now found she was to be monopolised elsewhere. It was just as well that I could not leave my job to go to the wedding because I might have broken down.

One strange feature of our war was the inland training-ship at Wetherby called HM Ceres. The Captain's name was Fanshawe and he took a fancy to my father, so frequently stepped out on Sunday afternoons and invited himself to tea. Two of his officers asked me to go with them to what was expected to be a good ship's concert. On arrival they gave me the totally shocking news that the Captain was furious when he heard that I was to be there. My car and driver had left before I knew this and my escorts then insisted I pay no attention to 'the silly old buffer'. At first he had said it would be bad for discipline for me to be led into the hall when all the men were seated, and after that argument had proved unsustainable declared that if anyone were to ask me to the ship it should be he and nobody else. When the time came, my companions supported me on either side and we waddled into the hall and to our seats. At the end of the performance the news was that the Captain planned to station himself at the door in a quite unprecedented manner, evidently to give me no chance of avoiding him. While I was wondering if he knew how hazardous it was to shake me by the hand in transit, he called out loudly: 'Good-evening, Felicity! *I* did not ask you here this evening.' Still flanked by my friends, but remembering my precarious balance, I controlled my feelings and thanked him benignly for the entertainment. My car had not yet returned so I stayed with the others in the Mess where I seen found that, having had his say, the Captain was trying to work his way round me. He did not succeed and I was thankful to get home and tell my father the whole humiliating episode. I felt ill-treated and very nettled but, even so, did not expect my father – the calmest of men – to take up his pen and write to the Captain to say that he would not have any daughter of his accused of gatecrashing when she was not. He ended his letter more characteristically with 'I hope your new potatoes were not nipped by the frost last night.' This letter brought a grovelling response, and that was the last we saw of Captain Fanshawe.

By the time the peacetime Secretary of the Marguerite Hospital returned, the office had got accustomed to hearing of my opinions on hunting and politics. My father had decided to retire from the Secretaryship of the Bramham Moor Hunt and it needed little persuasion from the Treasurer, Kenneth Parkinson, for me to take it on. In politics, I was in the wings waiting to be nominated chairman of the Barkston Ash Women's Conservative Association when the political embargo was lifted at the end of the war. So it was time to move on. Certainly members of the Hospital Management and House Committees had taught me a great deal. Always kind and considerate, they gave me a lovely pigskin bag as a leaving present.

By VE Day we had not got much bounce left for cheering. Village celebrations had to be borne and since Mill Hill made a splendid site for a bonfire it was there that the Walton effigy of Hitler went up in flames. The same treatment was given to an effigy of Hirohito, which now seems a little odd in view of his subsequent state visit to London.

5

Bramham Moor and Barkston Ash

In the job of Hunt Secretary my handicaps were unimportant and I was quickly put at ease by the Committee. My joint secretary being a fiercely keen and knowledgeable foxhunter, my work mainly entailed telephone, typewriter and taking minutes. Lord Harewood (father of the present Earl) was Chairman of the Hunt Committee and I was struck by his quick appreciation of detail in a situation with which he had been out of touch throughout the war, while the Hunt Committee was dormant.

At first I was not sure what to do about the chairmanship of the Barkston Ash ladies. I had formerly flirted mildly with the doctrines of both Socialism and Communism, partly with the wish to be different but also from a sneaking fear that Conservatives were too slow to respond to the needs of the people I had met amongst evacuees and parents of child patients at the Marguerite Hospital. Yet I was torn, because I respected the integrity and intellect of Conservative M.P.s more than those of other parties; on those grounds I justified accepting the invitation to allow my nomination to go forward, believing that those of us with busy and active minds should now get inside the party to try and stir it up and eradicate the smugness.

The election took place in the same upstairs suite of rooms where my pre-war speaking competition was held, so again there was the worry of how on earth to carry me up there. As usual, my mother and another staggered to the top and hauled me on to the platform. As Chairman, my aim was to learn all I could, so Hansard became my daily companion. I had lots of speaking dates and always tried to be short and sharp in my remarks, but I needed to garner all the expertise available. When I heard of a spring political school to be run by the Conservatives at Butlin's Holiday Camp at Filey, I made an immediate booking. It meant staying the week-end.

My mother gallantly accompanied me and I assured her that everyone would be looking out for us to help with our belongings, but when she got to the reception desk she was met by glum faces and doubts that we were even booked. When things at last got sorted out we were left to hobble several hundred yards in a gale before we could reach our chalet. We had not brought the chair for we had thought it would be unpopular with the Camp, so heaven knows how we managed. The chalet turned out to be a nasty little bedroom with thin walls and a bawling baby next door. Once we had gathered enough steam we went in search of the conference room. At last we found it, lurking behind a notice saying: 'Religious service in progress'. (This ruse was apparently, the only way to keep out the ordinary campers.) Later, we found bath and loo impossible to cope with, so made a quick dash for the Royal Crescent Hotel, Filey, just de-requisitioned. It was a welcome port of call and our unhappy memories were cast aside. The red and blue turkey carpet was still there. Back again at the political school I picked up a few useful wrinkles, but the week-end taught me that politicians with their noses set were not then inclined to give help and consideration to the halt and maimed in their midst. Having learnt that lesson, how crazy I was to plan to go to the Tory Conference at Blackpool!

When told that I could with full confidence put our bookings for Blackpool in the hands of a firm called 'Happy Holidays', I was stupid enough to believe it. They were given full details of my disablement and need for step-free accommodation. Trustingly we drove over there. Each time we stopped in Blackpool to ask where to find our hotel, we were sent further and further along the seafront. Finally, in semi-darkness and a raging wind, we saw the gleam of a swinging lantern illuminating the name we sought. The exterior was unprepossessing, but, sitting in the car, I felt things would be much better indoors. The door was opened to my mother by a welcoming lady in black satin, accompanied from the hall by a strong smell of Irish stew. A steep flight of stairs loomed up behind her. When a sudden gust of wind cut short my mother's opening remarks it also whistled all the hats off the hatstand, so the proprietress clutched my mother's arm to pull her inside and then close the door. There was no lift and no special ground floor room, nor had any mention been made of my requirements. The only porter was off duty and anyway suffered from a rupture. My mother's instinct was to head for home but, knowing my fanatical keenness to attend the Conference, without further ado hauled me up that steep staircase on my behind.

This did not end our Blackpool problems. Despite exhaustive enquiries, only on the last day were we told of an entrance on the level to the Winter Gardens, the scene of the Conference, so for three days my mother doggedly pulled and yanked me up what seemed like miles of steps and stairs to reach our seats on the balcony. We saw and heard little of the proceedings, for our time was chiefly spent navigating these hazards and I dreaded the thought of being asked for a report on my return. My mother wrote a roasting letter of complaint to those who had recommended

'Happy Holidays' and I decided never again to trust outsiders to make arrangements for us.

I was put on the list of the Yorkshire panel of speakers and went all over the county to address meetings at the rate of two or three a week. I had the advantage of combining three unusual features in the run of speakers – I was young (28 years old in 1946), a female and in a wheelchair. Presumably, the Labour Party knew I was tasting success for they started to send a blind man to my meetings, who sat in the front row and proceeded to heckle and question me soundly. No doubt this was designed to stop me getting the undivided sympathy of the audience. However, once I got used to him we became good friends and it was quite useful to have his questions to answer. People of many kinds and ages and from different districts kept on urging me to stand for Parliament; if not Parliament, they said, then at least I must aim for current affairs on radio or this new 'television.' As, above everything, I longed for a communication job that I could do well, it was little wonder that my ears pricked up at these flattering remarks.

My present occupations were a dead loss financially: a small honorarium from the Hunt and not more than £2, if I was lucky, for my political speeches. Petrol was paid for and my drivers varied between my mother, Prudence and the marvellous Fred. I knew that even were I to be elected to Parliament the pay was only about £600 per annum and would never cover the cost of the several helpers I should require, whereas there would be no pay at all while fighting a seat. What is more, I knew that Tories with independent means were then more popular as candidates with constituency selection committees. Against that, I felt sure that once my boat was pushed out there would be wonderful supporters to fill the financial gaps and I would be happy to sink my £2,500 capital, which was my only source of income. There was then no state benefit nor insurance for me, despite my six years of work at the Council Offices and the Hospital.

Our finances were so stretched that it was impossible to contemplate running a shop or a business, much as I should have liked to try such a venture, given my hospital experience in accountancy. A lack of funds was extremely restrictive at this point and, while I earned what I could, I racked my brains constantly for a suitable means of earning more.

Maybe because he had read reports of my meetings and activities, the editor of the *Yorkshire Post*, Linton Andrews, wrote and asked me to contribute a series of political articles for his front page, to be called, *Plain Facts*. This was very much to my liking and I received £36 for six articles. My spirit soared. A friend sent me this note from a former editor of the newspaper:

> I have to thank Miss Lane Fox, and I should imagine the Conservative Party in the north and indeed elsewhere owes much to her for her charm and cheerfulness and quite exceptional powers of political exposition. Her recent article in the Y. P. set out very pungently propaganda points likely to win converts to the Conservative cause. I wish her fine reasonableness more often took the place of less constructive attitudes.

Immediately, I wondered if journalism might be the right career for me? But accounts of cramped accommodation in the *Yorkshire Post* offices, and the need for writers to be able to get around, squashed that idea before it could develop. A miserable sense of failure lurked about me, not helped by well meaning people who regaled me with stories of recoveries achieved by other polio sufferers who, according to such accounts, not only got back to normal but started climbing mountains and performing other feats of strength. Only after careful quesitoning was it divulged that those wonders had generally been paralysed in only one leg or hand, or just in the back, so that to compare them with me was hardly fair. The name 'polio' was all we had in common. It was agonising to hear of these achievements, but I was confident we could have done no more to make me mobile for we had progressed a very long way.

The fact that I quite expected one day to have to be admitted to a residential establishment was not going to get me down, but the constant annoyance was the absence of any means of making my way in the world. Nevertheless, there remained the prospect of more magnificent race meetings at York and Wetherby! Racing and the book-makers provided a great interest and, with information supplied by good friends, I generally managed to keep out of deep water. A charming rascal introduced me to wagering mixed doubles, which on one occasion resulted in a coup of £400 for a ten shilling stake on Gordon Richards' mounts at Folkestone. Not every result was as lucrative, but at least the planning kept me busy.

One Sunday a flower vase broke in my mother's right hand and severed the main tendons of her fingers. Holding a roller towel round her hand, she managed to drive the car to the Marguerite Hospital from where she was immediately transported to Leeds and the General Infirmary. They operated and put her hand into plaster with wires like fish hooks attached to the injured fingers. She had barely come round when a misguided doctor told her that she must now realise she would no longer be able to look after me. If this did anything it was to strengthen her resolve, for as soon as she got home she found ways of coping with me without using that hand. A few very uncomfortable weeks later she was right back to normal, despite having two pretty groggy fingers.

In 1947 we all went to Filey again. Prudence took Maria, and Jimmy and Anne brought their sons Martin and Edward. We had my electric chair boxed over precisely to enable me to get on to the sands, so we were bitterly disappointed when, on the first day, I was ordered off by a bossy attendant. He said all motorised vehicles were forbidden on the beach unless they had special authority. Feeling angry and frustrated, we suddenly realised that our friend Jenks, the fisherman, was now an alderman, so we raced to him and soon got the necessary pass.

One day we found a tall, distinguished man examining my electric chair outside the hotel. This was Osbert Peake, then M.P. for a Leeds constituency, Conservative Minister of Pensions and later Viscount Ingleby. My chair interested him not only because of his Ministry but also on account of his son, Martin, who had lately contracted polio on service overseas with the Coldstream Guards. This meeting started a marvellous relationship with his whole family. For several days I drove my chair flat out down the beach to keep pace with Osbert's long stride, seizing every chance to pump him on party and political matters.

It was exciting to be told that I had been accepted onto the Conservative Central Office list of candidates. Although I recognised that the final selection for any seat depended on the constituency association, I knew that the candidate had to be approved at the centre, so this was one less hurdle for me on this difficult course. I was particularly pleased to hear that Iain Macleod had approved of me after my interview with him, for all that he said and wrote had an urgency, incisiveness and freshness to match the moment. He showed great insight and consideration for my difficulties. I was first selected and then discarded for a constituency that basically wished to adopt me but was persuaded otherwise because I was both a woman and a cripple. This was a hideous disappointment, in no way reduced by letters from County Officers with assurance that I had won my spurs and deserved a winnable seat. It was fortunate that these remarks meant little to me, for I heard no more. In retrospect I see their problems, but still maintain that in such circumstances it was wrong to raise my hopes.

The chairman of Barkston Ash was Geoffrey Smith, an able, intuitive, reticent managing director of a Tadcaster brewery. He understood my ambitions and frustrations, and appointed me to organise a constituency recruiting drive for the national campaign. Everyone worked like tigers and we produced a record result. Geoffrey's wife, Rosamond, was full of courageous political views and between us we proposed and seconded a resolution at a meeting of the Conservative Central Council in Central Hall, Westminster. We complained of the lack of suitable propaganda to catch the interest of the non-committed voter. Our remarks were surprisingly well received and we were almost overpowered by congratulations from politicians, audience and the press. My father telephoned to my mother and me in London to say that back home in Yorkshire he was pestered by press wanting details about me. We returned by train next day. Among our fellow passengers were members of a famous opera company who, as the train drew in to the platform in Leeds were not surprised to see that it was thick with press photographers. What certainly did surprise both them and me was that the photographers were not interested in the opera company but were waiting there for me.

Then I suddenly got a request from the Crown Film Unit to go with them to Oxford. They sent a car and this was a good way for my mother and me to dodge the petrol shortage and visit Jimmy and family. The official reason for this outing was for me to demonstrate on film a special chair, designed for me by a wonderfully kind inventor friend of the Loyds.

Jimmy and Anne were living at Barton House, Lockinge, and we arrived as they were in the middle of the second birthday party for Robin, their youngest child. My god-daughter, Jenny, was then aged four, and we went in to see them all having tea. I was standing talking to Catherine Loyd when I suddenly nose-dived and hit the floor with a blinding crash. All visiting adults looked terrified and gathered their children to them, no doubt thinking I was having a fit. The only mercy in this embarrassing situation was that I did not fall on any of the children. My knees were sorely damaged but the show had to go on. Next day I was filmed sitting down and standing up, helped by this magical chair – unfortunately with a look of agony on my face. The film won an international award and for a time was shown over here; a friend telephoned to say he had seen me at his local cinema and did not know what I was doing but thought I looked miserable. Many arthritic sufferers now benefit from that ingenious chair, the design of which has been used as a basis for many chairs with elevating seats.

It was excellent news for all of us when Tony Yates married Bobbie Nickols, war widow of Rodney Gold. She and I had recently worked together in Barkston Ash politics and we had all known and loved her since she was little. Prudence's in-laws gave her an attractive old house in Oxfordshire and she and Maria moved there. At the same time Nannie Holland decided to retire and live with friends in Nottingham where life, alas, did not turn out to be quite what she had hoped. So when Rosamond Smith told me that she could not go with Geoffrey to watch their horse,

Ridgewood, run in the 1949 St Leger Handicap because she had nobody with whom to leave their three children, I wired to Nannie and she at once agreed to come. Ridgewood won the race, I made £70 and Nannie was so proud of the part she had played that she might have been the jockey, Charlie Smirke, himself. Nannie was rewarded for being so co-operative and helpful by having a most happy last phase of nursery life during a long sit-in with the Smiths over the next few years.

Our vicar at home was a hilarious and good friend, so when he invited my mother and me to accompany him to a spiritual healing meeting in Leeds I did not put up my usual resistance. The speaker was Harry Edwards and, although I did not care for the hymn-singing or the enthusiastically pious atmosphere, he was a very impressive demonstrator. He visibly tired as he treated the patients called to the platform from the vast audience, and some appeared to benefit outstandingly. My hospital experience made me long to follow them home to see if the improvement was sustained. We just managed to speak to the great man, looking exhausted and in a hurry to catch a train south. He suggested I get in touch with the nearest spiritual healer, but the thought of a substitute did not appeal to me.

My father was diagnosed with a weak heart and, with difficulty, my mother persuaded him to give it a rest by staying in bed one full day a week. Although he started this routine most unwillingly, feeling guilty about what he had left undone, given his radio, a Peter Cheney book and the newspapers, he soon began to find there were advantages. It certainly helped to keep him active during the last years of his life. My mother took him to stay with Prudence for the Lord's Test Match and they loved their visit, except for a drive home which took seventeen hours owing to numerous prolonged breakdowns. Typically, my father remained quite calm throughout, obeying my mother's instructions to stay with the car while she walked miles up roads and garden paths searching for, and often finding, expert help, which enabled them to chug on a few miles until the petrol pump packed in again. He brought out his book and spectacles and made no complaint about having an unmolested read in the light of a full summer moon. At home, tension was high by the time they walked in at 6.00 a.m., but luckily I had with me an excellent helper called Alice.

A bye-election was called for the Wetherby division of the West Riding County Council. I jumped at the chance to have my name go forward, and on this occasion enjoyed a walk-over. County Hall was twenty miles away from Walton so it was asking a lot of the family in terms of transport, but as my father knew how desperately keen I was to get somewhere through my political efforts he offered to go with my mother when she drove me to meetings on at least one day a month, and that made all the difference.

The first day I attended County Hall we found seventy stairs and no lift. The staircase was wide with fairly easy treads, so my mother and a porter-cum-commissionaire picked me up and carried me to the top with zest and vigour. They had to leave me standing unsteadily at the top while they went back to carry up my chair and here I was greeted by a well-known left-wing County Alderman, who said: 'Ah, Miss Lane Fox I see! Now you will get the chance to learn that we are not all as black – or is it as red? – as we are painted in the papers!' I felt extremely small and ineffective and was anxious not to have to talk to anyone. Before long, however, Council members of all parties showed themselves kind and helpful to me, and the full Council gathering soon ceased to be frightening.

I was now an elected member of the Marguerite Hospital House Committee and found it interesting to have an inside knowledge of the other side of the fence. After the National Health takeover my old job had been divided among an administrative officer, an accountant, a hospital medical social worker and a Committee secretary. Certainly we had needed more staff to be able to do our work properly, but the present establishment really did seem to be overdoing it, especially as the bed occupancy had been reduced.

In October 1949, at seventy-five, my father had a severe stroke. It proved too much for his heart and he died the next day. He had been so unselfish, perceptive and above all, had contributed so much quiet wit and fun to our lives, that we all felt his loss dreadfully. My mother, though utterly bereft, maintained the calm exterior my father would have wanted. Beyond everything, he had detested any uncontrolled display of emotion and she continued to observe this stoicism with which they had supported each other through thick and thin for nearly forty years. To my shame, he had sometimes caught me being cross and unreasonable with my mother and had told me he would not have her treated with less than the gentleness and kindness to which she was accustomed. They were a truly devoted couple.

Decisions had to be made for the future and I was forced to agree that, if only for tax reasons, there were distinct advantages to accepting Prudence's hospitable invitation to us to share her Oxfordshire house. Not only was it lovely to have her with us, but as it now seemed unlikely that my mother and I together would have more than £900 a year on which to live, we obviously needed to cherish all the goodwill we could discover. It was the thought of being uprooted and starting again in a strange county that filled me with dismay. In Yorkshire I had begun to earn some standing through experience, and I knew and loved so many people there who were used to regarding me as fairly normal. Jimmy may have been right when he said it was about time I stopped behaving as if I were Queen of the May, but I doubt if he realised how much that tempo had helped to reduce the barrier of my physical dependence. The ice of my well-being was thin and the thought of having to resign from the County Council, Hunt Committee, Hospital Committee, all my Conservative appointments in the county and constituency, left me helplessly at square one. But my mother, at the age of nearly sixty, was facing up staunchly to the prospect of the move, so it was not for me to kick up a fuss.

The best news came from Osbert Peake. He suggested I get a wheelchair of a kind recently loaned to his son in an American design and which he felt sure would help me and those responsible for me. I tried it and agreed with him entirely. In every way it suited me better than any other model of chair, because it was light, manoeuvrable and comfortable, as well as folding away neatly. Everest & Jennings were exporting these chairs for which a US import permit was required. Although only £20 in the US it cost £100 over here, but when at last it arrived it proved well worth every penny. It gave me much more mobility and made me less complicated to handle. What is more, provided the big wheels were at the front – which they were not on most models – my weak shoulders could operate the self-propulsion and this gave me a new range of independence about the house. Osbert coped with the complicated permits and helped enormously in the whole successful exercise.

When my resignations were received I got tear-jerking letters in response which were a comforting expression of the esteem in which I was held. From the County Council it was unexpectedly pleasing to have the Labour Party's expression of belief that I had a contribution to make in social services from a non-partisan aspect. To my profound amazement and delight, the Bramham Moor Hunt presented me with a silver-gilt engine-turned dressing table set, engraved with the Hunt's crest by which to remember them.

My resignation from the Barkston Ash Conservative Association took place at Selby. They staggered me with a substantial presentation cheque. When they asked me how I would spend it, I told them I would have a portrait painted of my mother. Unfortunately, she did not take the matter seriously, and was reluctant to sit, but at last she relented and was painted by J.M. Teesdale. We were overwhelmed by the generosity of the gift.

We all worked like tigers to sell Mill Hill House at a worthy price, for now that the garden and shrubs had matured it began to look established. We finally sold to someone I met by chance at a political meeting.

When I am asked where I come from, I still say 'Yorkshire'. It is over 28 years since we left Walton but my roots are still there.

6

Trek South

The address of Prudence's house was The Fox, North Aston, Oxford. Built of mellowed Cotswold stone, it was long and low with a steeply pitched stone slate roof and attic windows. An oasthouse adjoined, an indication that The Fox had been a coaching house since Jacobean times. Its worst feature was that it stood beside a busy main road on a bad corner leading to the village.

When we began to live there we were accompanied by our daily cook and her housemaid sister who closed their house in Boston Spa in order to stay with us, and by a splendid Irish lady who came to help with me when Alice left to marry. Soon we realised that we would have to manage with less help, so while Oxfordshire neighbours longed to find staff willing to live in, we had to part with our treasures back to Yorkshire. Now my mother and Pooh somehow ran the house, coped with me, Maria and her dogs and pony, with daily help from the village on only two mornings a week. There was also Stanley Mobbs.

Stan came from an old North Aston family which had totally run to seed. He could hardly hobble and appeared a bit daft as well, but in the garden he had the green finger and a tame robin followed him about. He was an old age pensioner but could do all we needed as jobbing gardener. Stan stayed on the premises to caretake while a bathroom was built on to my ground floor bed-sitting-room before we moved in, but during these weeks he fractured his leg in a fall off his bike and had to go into hospital. This worked wonders for him, and old inhabitants told us he returned looking more kempt and spruce than he had for years. His dread was now that he might have to go back to his brothers in their hovel, so he pleaded to live in the outhouse above the garage where he kept the pea-sticks. Faced by his utter determination it was best to give in. When the weather turned cold he and his belongings moved into The Fox's good, dry attic and he gradually became integrated into the household. Talents acquired when he was in 'gentleman's service', as pantry boy to 'Earl Grey', now made themselves very useful, and on any day too stormy for garden work he cleaned the silver. He was not much older than my mother but when he saw her performing her feats of strength and agility, he wagged his head in the comfort of the pantry and said wistfully: 'She pops about wonderful for 'er age!' That remark had still more point when she 'popped' round the corner and found him enjoying an illicit nip of whisky in the dining-room.

When rationing ended, my mother and Prudence added to their repertoire of excellent dishes. The trouble was that for us there was still severe rationing by the purse, which obviously worried me in my capacity as the complete drone, for I could not think of any means to supplement the family's slender finances. Some disabled people managed to soar to success, but for me there seemed no prospect of obtaining the sort of training or financial backing to get me going.

My name had been placed on the Ministry of Labour's disabled persons' register when I finished work at the hospital and I had been told that this would help me when I needed a job, so I now contacted the Banbury office feeling curious but fairly confident.

The Disablement Resettlement Officer, however, took no time at all to tell me that my chances were nil. We lived fifteen miles from Oxford and eight miles from Banbury and the official mind did not expect severely disabled people ever to want to work if they lived so far away. No suggestions were forthcoming, even for any sort of training.

Once more the *Yorkshire Post* came to my rescue. Those faithful allies published a series of eighteen lighthearted anecdotal articles under the heading of 'Countrywoman'. In addition, feeling at the end of my tether, I circulated about fifty London publishers asking for work as a proof-reader, despite my lack of qualifications. It gave me a great boost to be taken on by Cassells; I thought they had been impressed by my letter until I heard that the reason for this break was my first name, which happened to be the favourite of the lady who opened my letter just when she was looking for a reader. The work was badly paid but it raised my spirits since being a proof-reader was something of a status symbol; at the same moment, a marvellous Yorkshire friend who knew of my worries supplied me with copy-typing for better money. Now life had a purpose and there was hope again.

Our new neighbours in Oxfordshire were very welcoming and we got to know a great many in a very short time. Life down there had a more feudal flavour and it often seemed that people had forgotten they were living in the second half of the twentieth century. It was all pretty and happy and comfortable, provided you did not think about it deeply. One brilliant bridge between the two eras was Lord Birkenhead. He took a great interest in my electric chair, so I later targetted him about the need for more progress to be made to counter polio. The epidemic in 1952 sent my nephew back from school in quarantine which shook me considerably and drove me to write an article for the *Yorkshire*

Post entitled 'Can we do more to fight poliomyelitis?' (This was published shortly before the wonderful news broke that a vaccine had been discovered). In an attempt to take the matter further I consulted Freddy Birkenhead. He considered the whole question carefully before recommending me to rope in the help of the man he thought possessed of the most truly compassionate and constructive outlook, Lord Longford, then Lord Pakenham.

To my mother's surprise, news of her hospital work preceded her south and she was asked to join the house committee of the then Wingfield-Morris Orthopaedic Hospital in Oxford – the scene of my filming adventure. The Duchess of Marlborough was chairman. As my mother made it clear from the start that she wished to take a very back seat, she was allotted a job in the dustbin area. Having quickly proved herself there, she was grabbed for duties at the top table.

My mother was also transferred unexpectedly to serve on the Magistrates' Bench at Deddington where she again found the Duchess of Marlborough, this time in the throes of arranging a great pageant at Blenheim. Princess Margaret and a bevy of glamour were staying at the Palace, but that did not prevent a message arriving at The Fox to tell us that seats would be reserved at the event for my mother and her 'chairborne daughter'. From that moment Mary Marlborough became our firm ally.

In addition to all these activities and her work on my behalf, my mother slaved away with Pooh reorganising the garden. Pooh was busily engaged as President of the Duns Tew Women's Institute and I was, for a time, her WI Hon. Secretary, which was both interesting and exasperating. My copy-typing job was no more than a pot-boiler, but the pot took so long to boil.

I wrestled with the nauseating thought that perhaps it was my rôle just to sit in the corner, never mind the frustration of such immobility, in order to be less trouble. The longstanding nature of disability took its toll both on me and those with me, but there were blessed friends who recognised this stage and tried to help. Clearly, it would be less selfish of me to draw back into the shadows and impose less on those of my family who did so much for me, day in day out. But it was just not in my character to do that, so I continued to rack my brain in search of ideas for remunerative employment. I dredged up memories of the Hospital auditors who had asked why I did not train for their profession. Injured jockeys built new careers armed with such a training, so why not me? The Hon. Treasurer of the Wingfield Hospital was the manager of an Oxford bank, and, as he was well known for being kind, wise and helpful, my mother asked his advice. She told him that I could not manage the loo without help and would have thirty miles to travel each day, but that we believed plans could be evolved to simplify this. He said, regretfully, that he could not recommend me to embark on such a course, partly because practically every Oxford building was infested with steps, and even when qualified I should continue to find these architectural features a barrier to future jobs.

Despondently, I wrote a piece of fantasy on village life and got it accepted for 'Woman's Hour'. The BBC invited me to read it. There was black ice on the roads the day I was due at the studio in Portland Place and my mother only just managed to keep the car on the road to London. In the studio I was surprised to be faced with, and told to speak into, a nasty looking object not unlike a wicker bedrest. The young lady producer told me that as I was a beginner they would not take it live but would record in case I fluffed my lines. Reassured, I started reading. When after the first two sentences, I was overtaken by a revoltingly fruity cough which had to be dealt with thoroughly and severely,

I was sure this would guarantee a re-take. At the end, to my consternation, the producer said the recording would go out unchanged as she thought it sounded nice and natural! Her attitude seemed distinctly anti-me. Luckily few friends heard the broadcast. The most apt response came from Brian Johnston on a postcard saying he was sorry not to have a bottle of cough mixture to send.

Jimmy gave me a subscription to a school of writing but short stories were its main subject and these proved beyond me. Kenneth Parkinson had a horse running at Ascot and it was marvellous to have such a favourite bit of Yorkshire to stay with us at The Fox. We went racing, and I forgot my troubles. He urged me to work again for the Conservatives and the Banbury Division co-opted me to their Executive Committee. Having noted the shortage of members in their constituency association and of funds, I saw that I must start a branch locally to try and supplement both.

When we had recruited a reasonable number of members to the new branch we had to keep interest alive, so we decided to hold a Brains Trust. The current editor of the *Sunday Times* lived in North Aston so we appointed him question master, with Major-General Sir Richard Lewis, Hester Knight (then chairman of the housing committee for her local authority), and Nicholas Hodson as members of the Trust. The Banbury Agent insisted on our inviting a Miss Margaret Roberts, unknown to us but a member of the Oxford University Conservative Association who had unsuccessfully contested Dartford at the General Election. We did not want her, but were pleasantly surprised when a blonde bombshell stepped off the 6.30 p.m. bus. We fed her a sausage and took her to meet her colleagues. My job was to plant searching questions amongst the thirty or forty members of the audience, but the moment each question was fired it was immediately answered, if not actually demolished, by Miss Roberts. Her answers were sound, clear and irrefutable. The others on the platform were left with nothing to do and only Hester caused a mild stir by keeping her King Charles spaniel on her lap throughout. She and I agreed later that after hearing Miss Roberts we would be loth to try and compete with her. We wondered vaguely if we should ever hear of her again, little suspecting that we had then seen and heard the future Rt Hon. Mrs Margaret Thatcher M.P.

My Everest & Jennings chair proved a godsend, so when an old friend of mine, Richard Wood M.P., became a Junior Minister at the Ministry of Pensions I was glad to go and explain its assets to the civil servants there. Richard was M.P. for Bridlington and had lost both legs below the knee in the war. My aim was to illustrate why this American chair did so much for me, whereas, I found the English models clumsy, uncomfortable and impossible to move. To greet me at the Ministry were about eight civil servants with stoney faces, each standing behind a wheelchair and looking resentful of my intrusion. No doubt they thought there was something in this for me, whereas all I wanted was to improve the locomotion prospects for so many unfortunate chairborne people currently using unsuitable chairs. These men loyally upheld the merits of their chairs, all of which were available on the NHS, while I argued that none but mine was right for me and that wherever I went in public people stopped me to ask how they might get a similar model. Was it fair, I asked, that because I had been able to raise the cash to buy it I could enjoy its advantages while others could not? Seven long years later the Everest & Jennings chairs were made available on the NHS, so I presume those unfriendly civil servants had moved away.

When Jimmy announced in 1953 that the firm of estate agents in which he was a partner was opening a branch office in Banbury,

I asked if I could have a job as stamp-licker. Having made the condition that there must be no tittle-tattle about the internal workings of the office which would be the responsibility of a manager, his answer was in the affirmative. I was untrained so would be entirely subservient and not expected to secure or enact business. I was very grateful for the chance and to try and repay him, did my best when well-intentioned friends brought me business to put in hand, little thinking that this would infuriate the manager, who became fiendishly jealous if clients asked for me. The office atmosphere became intolerable for, knowing that my lips would remain sealed, the manager tried every dirty trick in the book to get rid of me. My sitting place in the office was changed many times and always without consultation, and I ended up sitting in a through draught addressing circulars which I was pretty sure would never be posted. But my pay was £750 a year so I stuck it out for over two years.

News came of a clever car conversion which might just make it possible for me to drive. The major difficulty was how to raise the money to pay for the car to be converted, let alone how to meet the running costs. At this moment an extraordinary thing happened. My mother received a totally unexpected legacy – a relation she seldom saw died intestate and a considerable estate was divided among numerous cousins of whom my mother was one. Characteristically, she now told me to go out and buy a car though she knew, as I did, that the conversion must be made before it was known whether I would be able to drive. The conversion firm told me to find a secondhand Lanchester with a fluid flywheel – the forerunner of automatic transmission – and, when we had done so, adapted it to be driven without having to use either foot and with my arms propped to steer, accelerate, brake and control. I was particularly keen to drive because it

Felicity, pre-polio, in 1926

The portrait painted of Felicity in 1958 by J M Teasdale

Felicity in about 1963

Felicity drove everywhere in this chair, not realising for many years that she needed a licence to drive it!

Felicity at a family wedding in Durham, December 1968

Felicity and her mother, Enid Lane-Fox, in their flat at Marlborough Court

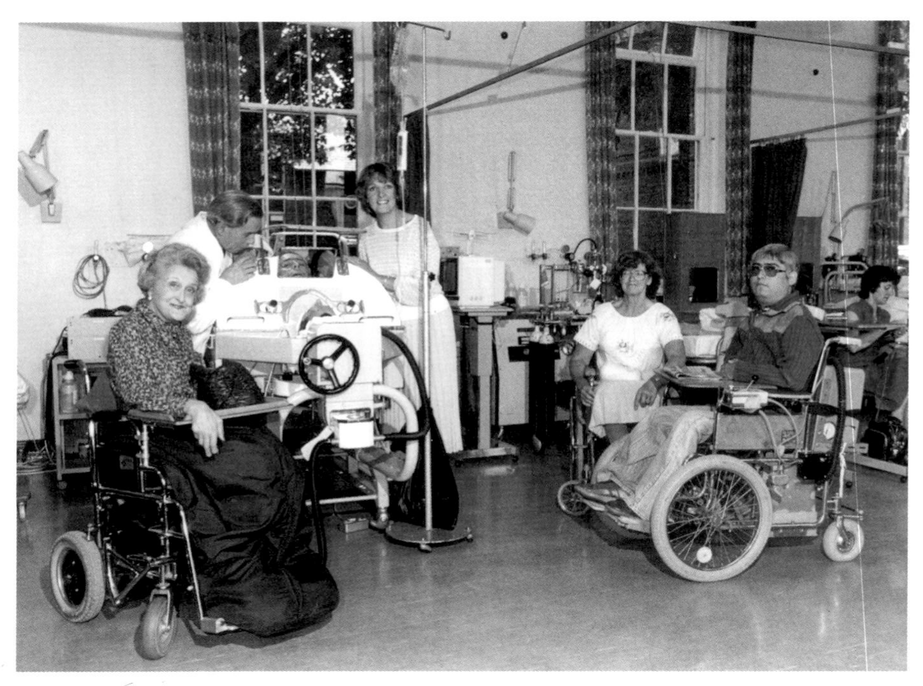

Phipps Ward, Clapham. Felicity is on the left and the actress, Penelope Keith, is in the centre. Penelope became a patron of the St Thomas's Hospital Lane-Fox Unit, named after Felicity

One of the last photographs of Felicity, taken between 1986 and 1988

would make me more useful for the office, so when the model was ready I got a week's leave and went to London with the car to attend the British School of Motoring in Chelsea, where there was a special department which dealt with disabled drivers. At first the instructors were despondent about my chances, but after a week of concentrated tuition I happily drove my mother back to Oxfordshire. For the next three months we spent many hours practising on a disused airfield. Then I took my driving test. It gave me enormous satisfaction to pass the test first time.

Although I could now drive myself to work each morning there was the problem of transferring me from car to chair. Colleagues in the office helped to get me and the chair out of the car until this became too much of an imposition, so I appealed for help to the St John's Ambulance Brigade. They responded magnificently at first, but as the novelty wore off help became spasmodic and frequently I had to try and lure helpers from their headquarters and often pursue them round the town. I knew it was asking a lot of them but there really was no alternative.

Now that I had the car, it sometimes suited the office for me to escort clients to properties. Once I led a glamorous young Greek shipping tycoon all round Oxfordshire. As he followed me up hill and down dale in his high-powered car I prayed fervently that the electric button (on which my gimcrack gear change depended) would hold out. I showed him countless houses but none caught his fancy and he never, ever smiled. Another taxing outing was when I fetched a very weird man from the London train and took him to see a lady who was selling her house. This prospective purchaser was highly nervous with long hair, a beard and very long, dirty fingernails. I found him distinctly disconcerting before we reached the house and am ashamed to say that, as I left him with the unfortunate lady, I was delighted not to be able to get out of the car. Having lunched at home, I returned to take him to the train to find the lady by now very scared. She told me he was smoking strange smelling cigarettes and had requested her, quite seriously, to lock up his sandwiches in her safe! My car flew him back to the station. Needless to say, he did not buy the property. After this incident I decided that I would never again drive around the country alone with a 'nut case', even if it cost me my job.

Eventually the office manager became positively belligerent and, not surprisingly, my health broke down under the strain, especially as my arrangement with Jimmy forbade me to tell him of my troubles. When I retired, well and truly hurt, the manager came out to The Fox and said he wished to apologise to me. Knowing the facts, however, my mother would not allow him to see me. Maria's usually docile dachshund took the law into her own hands, sneaked up behind him and bit him firmly in the back of the leg, tearing his trousers.

In hospital, I was glad to discover that for the first time since I was twelve the scales showed only eight stone. My worries had also deprived me of the ability to sleep. While at first I did not connect this with my weight, the doctor made me eat up and I then found that I quite soon recovered. So, alas, I was not intended to stay thin.

A rather solitary member of the Bramham Moor Hunt Committee was William Spooner, who had lost his wife and his only child within six months of each other early in the war. He was the son of the late Warden of New College, Oxford, known, amongst other things, for his 'spoonerisms'. William had inherited both his father's speech impediment and his clear thinking. He had built up an engineering works at Ilkley and combined a dedication to making business happy and successful with a love of the arts and fondness for horses. He was a great philanthropist and continued to be kind to me even after we moved south. Now, when he heard I had been having a rough time, he took me off to stay with his sister and brother-in-law at Cadlington House near Petersfield. This was the first time I had stayed away without my own helper, but the driver of William's Rolls, George, quickly changed from chauffeur to keeper for me. They had cleverly arranged for the lady who usually laid out the dead to dress and undress me and she proved to be excellent and dealt with me quite easily. I was given a bell to ring at night, but heavier than I could manage so it was just as well no break-ins or emergencies occurred.

It became a popular topic for some tactless, if well-meaning, people to ask, as my mother would soon be too old to look after me, what I proposed to do about it. I was flattered that at least they thought me capable of discussing the subject, but it would have been more constructive if they had had some scheme or suggestion to put forward. I doubted if they really cared deeply about what I planned for myself as long as I was tidied away. This prompted me to apply for a vacancy in the Cheshire Homes but I was much relieved when my mother and Pooh declared themselves strongly opposed to this idea. Obviously, I was far better looked after at The Fox than I could be elsewhere, though if there had been a centre which offered career prospects I would have gone there like a shot. I had a permanent guilt-complex about being considered a slave driver, and resented the lack of useful and remunerated occupation for me. Pooh angelically provided me with a comfortable home and all that went with it, but I seemed to be stagnating and still pined for Yorkshire where I believed my chances would be better.

A man who was severely paralysed reported that when he left

the Wingfield Hospital he got good results from staying with two spiritualists in East Grinstead, so, helped by a kind friend, I went down there. Living conditions for me there looked a bit basic so I did not tell my family too much. It was a ghastly struggle to get me up to a first floor bedroom. Ramshackle oil heaters on the landing were in imminent danger of being knocked over, particularly by one of the ladies who spent the nights walking up and down in a semi-trance. When I had been there for two days snow fell heavily and the walls of my bedroom became covered with damp patches and the room freezing cold. The icy atmosphere permeated my whole being so that it became a physical effort just to try and think straight. Every morning I was wheeled in my chair to the garage where I was transferred to the car in which I toured the neighbourhood in icy and difficult conditions. The ladies really did seem possessed of supernatural powers and my whole life appeared to be an open book to them. While I was grateful to them, I was a little intimidated and feared falling under their spell. My nerve went after ten days and that morning after they had gently put me into my car, expecting me back at teatime, I bolted hell for leather the 130 miles home. My mother and Pooh drove me back to East Grinstead the next day to collect my belongings. This was one more failure to chalk up, and I blamed myself for not having been strong enough to withstand the soul-searching technique employed by my enigmatic hostesses, whom I believed to be genuine and good. If the weather had been better and my resolve stronger, things might have been different.

Once again the *Yorkshire Post* took my articles and I was delighted with these two letters. The first was from the Editor:

> Thank you very much for sending me the delightful article 'It's almost worth a guinea a minute'. You almost persuaded me that

> I ought to go chasing a fox . . . I am very glad to have you as one of our contributors. Women readers must get tired of the eternal fashion and cookery notes. It is refreshing to have your woman-in-the-country articles.
>
> Yours sincerely, (signed) LINTON ANDREWS

The second was from an illustrious contributor:

> As a reader of, as well as a writer for, the *Yorkshire Post*, may I say how very much I enjoyed your piece this morning. I have seldom read anything which conveyed the atmosphere of the racecourse so delightfully. It reminded me of the wonderful descriptions in Siegfried Sassoon's *Memoirs of a Foxhunting Man*. I love these country pieces and wish so much that I could write them but I am afraid I am completely urban minded!
>
> Yours sincerely, (signed) DERRICK BOOTHROYD

These welcome words encouraged me so that I was inspired to write a letter to the *Sunday Times* which was published in the edition of 20th November, 1956. At the Hospital that week we ran into the Professor of Orthopaedics, Professor Joseph Trueta. He was entirely in favour of what I had proposed in my letter and promised to respond to it. In addition, he took up the theme of my plea and approached the National Polio Research Fund who subsequently agreed to contribute £50,000 towards setting up the kind of centre to which I had referred. During the next six years the Professor worked with unlimited dedication to get the scheme over every kind of pitfall and right through to completion.

Bill Yates – married, divorced and about to re-marry – called at The Fox and told us that as the director of the Harewood

Three-Day Equestrian Event he wanted help. My mother had little difficulty in getting him to employ me in a secretarial capacity. Monna Rudé agreed that I could stay with her in Leeds, which with my car was within easy reach of Harewood. It all worked well. When I arrived each day one of several people would trans-ship me and wheel me into the little wooden hut in Harewood Park that was Bill's office. Spare time up there provided me with a longed for chance to drive around old haunts and see the people I missed so much.

My mother joined me in Yorkshire for the Event week and on the evening before it began she wheeled me round the stalls already set up. To our embarrassment we ran straight into the Princess Royal who nevertheless, appeared glad to find some familiar faces. Ever since Her Royal Highness had come to Yorkshire she had been close friends with my mother who sometimes stood in as her lady-in-waiting, and as children we had known her many kindnesses. Now when the buses tore up and down the drive beside us HRH stepped off the grass towards them. For a moment I thought she would command them to slow down, but instead she took up her position with her back to the drive and faced us, saying: 'I will *not* allow them to run over you! After all, I am *President* of this event and surely they would not dare to run over their President.'

For the cocktail-party at Harewood House I managed without a chair but met there the hazardous slippery floors which became still more treacherous when, as usual, my mother and I were greeted by the Princess with an affectionate kiss which all but knocked me off my delicate balance. When Her Royal Highness asked how life was going for me in the south, I replied that I had a nagging wish to try and buy a bungalow in Yorkshire and return north. She looked serious and said: 'Before you take such a step it is important that you should know what job you want to do when you get here.' This bit of unwelcome realism pulled me up short and illustrated how extremely practical she was, despite her sheltered surroundings and privileged upbringing.

While I was in the north the Yorkshire Association for the Care of Cripples asked if I would once more become their fund-raiser as they needed money to set up a residential training-school and sheltered workshop. They were converting an ex-police orphanage in Harrogate and wanted me to occupy a staff flat in the establishment. The sum to be raised was £30,000 and I agreed to move in and do my best. It was wonderful to be needed.

My mother and Prudence faithfully accompanied me from Oxfordshire to settle me in and stayed the night in Harrogate, feeling slightly apprehensive about me. While I assured them I would be OK and felt this might be the very job for me, my car had different views. I drove to see them off from their hotel, and on the way the car sat down. The electric button of the gear-change had conked out. That settled it. Leaving my car to be repaired, we all squeezed into Pooh's small van and returned to The Fox. My new employers accepted an arrangement whereby I mounted an appeal for the Yorkshire Association from Oxfordshire and we were all amazed by the incredibly generous response from friends and acquaintances. We went to Harrogate for a large meeting addressed jointly by Sir Leonard Hutton, my cousin Elizabeth Cayley, and me. Several lesser functions were also held at different points in Yorkshire. Very soon we netted £18,000, with a further £12,000 in the bag. Our car was seldom off the road between Oxfordshire and Yorkshire, but at least the Association's St George's House began to look like business.

Back in Oxfordshire I visited the DRO and was in no way surprised to find he had no suggestions for me as to training or jobs. Nevertheless, this reawakened my feelings of bitter disappointment and frustration. There was no shortage of social activities, including Christmas parties with Jimmy and Anne and their family who now lived just ten miles away but no matter how much I enjoyed these excellent gatherings, I was plagued by a nagging sense of dissatisfaction at doing nothing to justify all the efforts made on my behalf.

My left foot had bothered me for some time, so in 1957 Professor Trueta decided to operate. The Wingfield Hospital was now called the Nuffield Orthopaedic Centre and that is where he straightened three toes and crossed a tendon in my leg. The object was that this would make it easier for me to wear shoes. I was admitted to a private bed where they were shocked to find that my rate of breathing measured only 700 instead of the required 2,000. Blow as I would I could not drive the spirometer needle any higher. Till then I had dismissed my breathing difficulties as a boring inconvenience but now they were taken very seriously. Once the operation was over I was put on a kind of respiratory belt which soon helped a lot. Unfortunately, my digestion went to pieces after the operation and I felt wretchedly sick for at least four weeks. They gave me every sort of test and only by chance discovered that whenever pethidine was given to reduce the pain of my toes, the blinding faintness and sickness reappeared. From then on the words ‘no pethidine’ have been emblazoned on my heart.

To be in hospital over Christmas certainly has its points. Carol-singing in the dark wards lit by storm lamps held by young nurses in uniform accompanied by medical students, all directed in their singing by an Oxford college organist, was unforgettable. My mother visited me often, which brought from Matron the slightly caustic comment: ‘You have a most devoted visitor.’ She could say that again! I had lots of callers, including a very welcome visit from Sir Oliver (now Lord) Franks. His was the most diplomatic visit of all, which, considering his career, was understandable. He arrived when a nurse had arranged to rub my back with surgical spirit but, having bared my backside, had failed to lock my door. Sir Oliver, wise man that he is, took not the slightest notice. He just sloped over to the armchair and engaged me in scintillating conversation.

We changed my car with all the concomitant complications. I got an Austin Westminster because it was the smallest car with automatic transmission made in this country at that time. It seemed huge and powerful after my first car and made light of long journeys. The steering was also easier – except when it came to parking, which was ghastly. Driving was now full of fun and dash.

During the 1959 General Election campaign I did a stint as press officer for our M.P. As representative of our constituency on the Wessex Provinical Area Council, I could do no less. When all was over, my mother noticed that once more a glaze had fallen over my eyes. She made the electrifying and, to me, absolutely marvellous suggestion that we might go to London and see if anybody at Central Office could make use of my services. A chance to live in London was what I wanted.

7

Uses and Abuses

William Spooner provided just the help we needed by lending us his flat in Dorset Square, NW1. There was a savage little flight of steps to the front door but we generally managed to enlist lifting assistance from unsuspecting passers-by. In retrospect it seems extraordinary that on our first visit to Smith Square we got lost in the network of one-way streets. My over-anxiety did not help. Soon after our arrival I was absorbed into the Central Office press cutting section and worked there voluntarily until Christmas. The Director of Conservative Research Department, Michael Fraser, promised to tell me if a suitable vacancy occurred in the Research Department.

There were arrangements to be made if I was to go on working in London. My mother got us a furnished flat in Marsham Court where we were joined by Harriet Hare. Harriet had turned up at the Nuffield Centre to do her orthopaedic training and having decided not to become state registered, she agreed to look after me instead. When we made that plan I had lived in Oxfordshire and it was very kind of her still to come to me now that I had moved to London. She quickly learnt to cope, so my mother returned to The Fox and, every Friday evening, I drove down there with Harriet. She soon found life dull without a dog so stepped out one day and bought 'Candy' from Battersea Dogs' Home.

I have to admit that, despite coming as I do from a dog-loving family, I have never been ecstatic about our canine friends. It may be because I cannot let them out when they whine and look appealing, or perhaps just that I am too selfish. I tried hard with Candy, poor thing, though she started to gulp with car-sickness even before the car began to move. Said to be a Manchester terrier, she was really a mongrel who ran wild at the sight of the country. No part of the precious garden at The Fox was safe from her frantic digging and even dog lovers like my mother, Prudence and Maria had to admit she was a bit of a menace. Harriet would not countenance the faintest criticism of her, so feelings ran high as Candy tore wildly through the flowerbeds.

Having been loosely connected with the appeals committee of the National Fund for Polio Research for a year or two, I now decided to ask them about a job. The Director explained at length that since I had no training or expertise to offer (apparently my four years' work in hospital did not count), it would be tricky to find anything suitable. I felt very small and now wonder how such a dispiriting situation could have been allowed to arise in those surroundings, for this was the sort of treatment I expected only from the DRO. By now I was blubbing against my will, when to my joy was told of an eight-week research job which was to start in January. The Director said that in view of my lack of qualifications, he could not offer me more than £7 per week in an exercise that would be to search reference books published both nationally and internationally for information likely to be useful for inclusion in Selwyn Goldsmith's forthcoming work, *Designing for the Disabled*. When published this became the standard UK reference book on the subject. During the course of my short job towards its preparation I spent days at the Royal Institue of British Architects in Portland Place and at the Building

Centre at Watford. My mother drove and assisted me to move from car to building whenever necessary. Having been nettled by the implied suggestion that my labours were worth nothing I worked especially hard to complete the substantial task within the appointed time. The office in which I collated the findings was renowned for its poor ventilation and I am certain that its atmosphere contributed to the sharp attack of pneumonia I suffered before leaving.

Once recovered, I was interviewed and given a filing and annotating job at Conservative Research Department, which carried a thrilling salary of £12 rising to £15 a week. The worst aspect of it was that the lady establishment officer had a built-in hatred of my wheelchair. She complained that its wheels dirtied the carpet, that it took up space she needed (which had not been occupied before), that she could not leave its occupant without a telephone in case of fire and for this reason must deny an instrument to the leader of the Party. She harassed me about every aspect of office accommodation and never failed to emphasise what a heavy encumbrance I was. As far as I could, I ignored her remarks.

Then Harriet decided she must leave me for something more interesting. While it was lovely to have my mother with me again, I felt guilty about it. So when a talented and attractive temporary secretary was provided to help with my job, I asked if she would look after me in return for her keep and lodging and a tiny wage. She accepted. Called Prudence, she was a Canadian art student who quickly found out how to dress me and put me to bed, organise my bathroom activities, and do the shopping and cooking. She rode a motor bike and was an excellent, if furious, driver of my car. Pru and I developed a good give-and-take relationship whereby if she had a date I went to bed at 6.00 p.m. and was contacted by her throughout the evening from nightclubs or wherever she happened to be, knowing she would return in a flash if necessary. The wheezes were always hovering about, so much so that my doctor sent me to a hypnotist who specialised in curing asthma, but without success.

Pru generally chose to stay in London at week-ends so I drove alone to Oxfordshire on Friday evenings. The car never let me down, though the wind-screen wipers once gave up the ghost in the middle of a rainstorm, rendering visibility nil. There were strings of cars behind me on a narrow road, other drivers becoming infuriated as I groped about blindly and blocked their way home. Suddenly, a car squeezed past and pulled up directly in front. The driver jumped out to tell me he had diagnosed my trouble and proposed driving slowly ahead towards Bicester so that I could stick to his tail. For the next twenty miles we went at a snail's pace; when the rain stopped he waved his hand out of the window and just disappeared into the night. Someone sprang to my assistance again when at traffic lights on Western Avenue a lorry on my left pulled straight across me as the lights turned green, practically scraping my car and making me brake hard. The others chased him and edged him into a lay-by to deliver a lecture on inconsiderate driving. I had used the 'disabled driver' badge reluctantly but now saw it paid welcome dividends.

I generally managed to take my leave to coincide with York Races. We had marvellous visits to the Parkinsons, and this was a great chance to see friends, old and new. One of the latter with special appeal was Sue Masham, in a wheelchair after breaking her back in a point-to-point some years earlier. She and her husband had built a charming one storey house of Georgian design; all the kitchen, bath and work areas were planned for use from a wheelchair. In addition, she had devised her own way to ride a horse, and, having very strong arms, drove both cars and chairs at high speed and was thus extremely independent. Having been active in sport all her life, while at Stoke Mandeville Hospital Spinal Injury Unit after her accident she became a paraplegic swimmer and table tennis player of high standard. It was excellent to discuss with her aspects of our mutual problems which meant little to the able-bodied. Her light-hearted dismissal of her own problems belied her generous concern for other disabled people whom she genuinely longed to help. With her constructive attitude it was absolutely right she be created Baroness Masham of Ilton, which enabled her to take an active part in the House of Lords and raise the profile of all disabled people.

My mother was now Chairman of the Nuffield Orthopaedic Centre's House Committee. In 1962 she received a letter from Lady Hamilton, wife of the industrialist, Sir Patrick Hamilton, asking permission to build an experimental house for disabled people in the grounds of the hospital. Knowing this was a matter for the Regional Board, she arranged a meeting and was interested to note the quiet determination with which Lady Hamilton won her way. Having heard this story I was particularly interested a few weeks later to meet the lady at a London meeting, a valuable step towards achieving my dream of obtaining better provision for disabled people.

After being with me for nearly two years, Pru returned to Canada. Only then was it divulged that she had never hitherto stuck to a job and had been the talented despair of all her well-wishers. We had got along well together and when she left she arranged a temporary replacement in the form of a charming Canadian trained nurse. While she was with me I was elected Vice Chairman of the Wessex Area Women's Advisory Committee so we travelled anywhere from Banbury to Dorset, or Buckinghamshire to the

Isle of Wight. Our quarterly meetings took place in the Overseas League Club in St James's and much scaling of stairs was entailed to reach the appointed room; the only possible route for me to be carried up by was by the iron fire escape with its twenty steps.

Stair-climbing was an inherent part of attending political meetings and we learnt to practise stair-avoiding tactics. The Oxford Town Hall had at least seventy stairs which had to be tackled to attend the Banbury Divisional meetings – until we discovered a lift behind the Mayor's parlour. In that way we got a straight run through to the Council Chamber. As the meetings were held on Saturdays the family found it a drag to wait about for me in Oxford, although my mother once underestimated the duration of our meeting, with surprising consequences. When she arrived early to fetch me, she peeped through the little window in the door to the Chamber, spotted me and could not resist opening the door a chink to try and catch my eye to make me laugh. There were sixty or so people between us, so it was impossible for me to wave to her to go away. I was aghast when an earnest young lady sprang to her feet to announce in conspiratorial tones: 'My Lord Chairman, we are being overheard! There are strangers at the door!' With this, the Agent and a young farmer flew to throw open the doors, only to reveal there Mrs Lane Fox, looking all innocence. She was well known to most people present so was ushered into the hall where free seats were scarce, but when one was at last found for her she sat down looking unusually abashed, knowing she had been caught redhanded in this characteristic bit of her mischief. She glanced sheepishly in my direction, I glared back.

At last my dream of a centre to advise and inform disabled people at the Nuffield Orthopaedic Centre, Oxford, was realised and Professor Trueta received permission to call it Mary Marlborough

Lodge. Unfortunately, its namesake became desperately ill before the opening ceremony and could take no part, so my mother made the official approaches which resulted in the late Duchess of Kent performing the official ceremony. Field Marshal Lord Harding, chairman of the Fund which contributed the money, was the principal speaker and I was proposer of the vote of thanks to Her Royal Highness. My old letter to the *Sunday Times* had been selected for hanging in the hall of the Centre to illustrate the origins of the idea to set up the establishment. I was therefore expected to explain what prompted me to write my letter. I told of seeing cripples sitting in dreadful old wheelchairs on pavements as we passed through the streets of Leeds on my way to physiotherapy sessions in the 1930s. Many were polio cases and looked forlorn and dejected in both their physiognomy and attire, and I felt sure that with the right help and advice their lives could have been greatly enhanced. It had been my hope ever since to preserve others from their sadness and the new centre could do so much in this way. Her Royal Highness spoke charmingly of her wish to see disabled people helped towards a better chance to become self-supporting and to participate more fully in life.

Shortly afterwards my path crossed again with that of Princess Marina when Lady Hamilton asked me to show visitors around a display house which she and the Central Council for the Disabled had set up in Victoria. There I had to demonstrate the remote control devices supplied to prove how daily living could be made much easier for severely disabled people. Even though the button refused to function to open the curtains, Her Royal Highness clearly got the message and contributed some deeply practical comments about the purpose of the exhibition. A great many people toured the show and I found that physios, occupational therapists, social workers were all as surprised as I was by the effects of good equipment. Now for the very first time I was able to turn on a gas cooker, to hang washing on a line and even to reach the back of a cupboard.

While I was doing this job the Central Council for the Disabled asked me to make their BBC TV appeal. It was to take place in three months' time and I was invited to take part in a strictly voluntary capacity. Having always regarded the Council as too woolly to be useful, I now felt in a weak position to take it on. However, Lady Hamilton encouraged me by assuring me that a good response would help her endeavours, so I accepted on condition that I could write my own script based on the findings of the Disabled Living Activities Group of which Lady Hamilton was chairman. It worried me to hear that senior officials in the CCD feared that the appeal would be a flop if delivered by an unknown amateur, but my mother averted my approaching Slough of Despond by sending hundreds of postcards to generous and kindhearted friends telling them of my appearance. What we had not bargained for was my severe attack of pneumonia which knocked me flat three weeks before the day, and caused the doctor much concern. When I was beginning to recover, being in bed gave me time to write and master my script.

Virtually recovered by the appointed night, I went with my mother to the BBC Television Centre in a sumptuous limousine. We were shown to a luxurious dressing room and fed a delicious 'champagne dinner'. A kitchen scene had been constructed and, with the minimum of talk, I showed its amazingly helpful elements. The sum of £12,500 which poured in afterwards amazed everyone, for it was amongst the very highest totals subscribed that year to television appeals. The 6,000 letters included many from friends, some from long ago, and the whole correspondence made me aware of the generosity and goodwill which could be harnessed to help schemes that could be shown to be really useful and genuine. The Central Council seemed satisfied, for they appointed me a Vice President.

I dearly wanted to settle in London. My mother promised that while I was at work she would take on the impossible task of trying to find an inexpensive base, which had no front door steps, was either on the groundfloor or had a lift, with central heating and porterage, if possible. We agreed that her chances of success were slim. She consulted five estate agents unsuccessfully, then found herself outside Harrods in a rainstorm. She decided to tease them with her requirements and was amazed to be told of a fifth floor flat in a block, with one shallow step at the entrance and a good lift. It comprised a large sitting-room, hall-dining area, two bedrooms, bath, loo and kitchen. I rushed to see it and immediately fell in love with it. It was well planned to take my chair and I was quickly enchanted by the wide view over the chimney tops. We took a base for three years and then for a bit longer, until finally we bought a longish tenancy. It has proved to be a wonderfully happy place to live and even turned into quite a good investment. Undoubtedly No. 30, Marlborough Court was one of my mother's most inspired finds. Local shopkeepers and tradesmen soon took her to their hearts and, despite the fact that she was by then pretty hard of hearing, she quickly made friends. We continued to return to The Fox at week-ends, however.

Our local garage proprietor in Oxfordshire invited me to visit the gliding club to which he belonged, to see for myself the good work being done there to provide London teenagers with an outlet for their high spirits. Prudence accompanied me one Sunday morning, on which occasion we were both totally nonplussed to be greeted by six keen gliding fellows, all dead set on carrying me bodily into a glider. This had not been our plan at all and we were even less keen when we saw the crudely constructed machine. However, there was nothing to do but fall in with their schemes and I soon found myself sitting in the seat in front of the 'pilot'. It reminded me of the old Bleriot-type planes, with no roof or sidescreens, just a talc windscreen. They put a large pair of goggles on me and told me not to move my feet on the pedals, which was a bit ironic. Looking down, I was disconcerted to see daylight between the slats of wood under my feet. The club was based on an old airfield so we were winched at tremendous speed and with a deafening noise for several hundred yards. When at last we were airborne my senses were in turmoil. I kept eyes tight shut, so I was unable to respond to the pilot's instructions to look at the harvest and the beauties of the countryside. Clearly they felt I should be glad of this chance to fly around in silence, unfettered by physical handicaps. After three agonising minutes we returned to earth and I mentally vowed never, under any pressure, to leave the ground in such a machine again. This was the first time I had ever flown. My worry was not to appear ungrateful to the helpers whose idea it had been and who had lifted me on board. My display of gratitude completely hoodwinked Pooh, who said that, as I had obviously enjoyed it so much, she too must go for a spin. No secret sign from me would dissuade her and it was almost a relief to see she had turned bright green when she returned. By the time we got back to The Fox we both looked total wrecks and neither could face lunch.

When the Wessex Area Women's Advisory Committee needed a new chairman, my wheelchair tugged at their heartstrings and got me elected. My opponent undoubtedly had brains, charm and good looks, and if I had had to vote she would have been my choice. So I was not surprised to hear that as Pooh came to collect me she ran into two ladies wagging their heads in disappointment over the election result. The appointment brought coveted perks in the form of automatic membership of the Party's National Women's Advisory and of the National Union Executive Committee, among other things.

Wessex took quite a toll of us at week-ends, when either my mother or Pooh would rush me up the road to meetings as far apart as Southampton, Oxford, Salisbury, Bournemouth and Portsmouth. My Hillman car stood up valiantly to the battering, but one Saturday evening sat down with my mother and me on Newbury Downs beyond East Ilsley where there was no garage open to help us. In our desperation we discovered that we could make the car go if we went up the hill backwards. In this fashion we climbed to the highest point and then daringly turned round, only to find that the car now took charge as though it were jet-propelled. As with time and tide we could wait for no man, not even for the traffic lights in Oxford, and we flew on to The Fox where we drew up panting, amidst clouds of smoke.

When my 'searches' for Michael Fraser were finished, he kindly arranged to transfer me to the Home Affairs section, which dealt with the subjects that interested me. The pity was that this meant using another house, with awkward front door steps and a perishing lack of central heating. Plans were made for us to enter from the other side which took us to the basement where there was a lift to the groundfloor, but the lift was too small for my chair. To solve this problem I was hauled to my feet to wobble up in the lift before my chair was brought up in a second load. This placed a great strain on my mother and Prudence, particularly when we had coats and rugs and mackintoshes to carry, and the establishment officer never missed a chance to point out what a nuisance it was to have me there. Tables and equipment were continually moved about overnight to make it highly inconvenient for me to work in my chair. My mother cared more about my well-being than for anyone's disapproval, however, and firmly imported a paraffin stove for winter and a desk fan for summer, which greatly improved the badly ventilated atmosphere.

The nature of my work had now become boringly insignificant and, looking back at the trials involved, I can't think why I stayed. It was not a happy atmosphere now and I worried when I saw the lack of Party loyalty displayed by several of the second flight members of staff. In 1964 when the Labour Party won the Election, changes took place in the Department. Michael Fraser – one of the few people who was truly astute and had the interests of the Party truly at heart – was transferred to Smith Square to become Vice Chairman of the Party. A new Director was appointed who told me that in the intensified work programme there would no longer be room for me and my chair. I had been there five years and made no complaint when they were good enough to give me three months' pay.

Work on the disablement front forged ahead and for a time Lady Hamilton used me as minute secretary for her advisory panel, which finally formed the Disabled Living Activities Group. Her leading Committee members included Professors Titmus, Schilling, and Tizard, Drs Wigley, Bach, Sommerville and Holt, and architects Ronald Fielding and Felix Walter, plus high-ranking observers such as Mr Tatton Brown. Before long the title, establishment and function were changed to become the Disabled Living Foundation, with Miss Stow as the Director and its headquarters at 346, Kensington High Street. Now, apart from generous and important voluntary contributions, this important foundation receives grants from Government and per capita payments from local authorities. It is visited by Cabinet Ministers, and consulted by professional bodies, disabled people and helpers.

It was the end of an era of perpetual childhood when Nannie Holland died. She had come to live in an old people's home in Oxfordshire from which she could spend at least one full day a week at The Fox; she died after a short stay in hospital. She had had a great talent for recounting the past and stories of her early life were favourites with all of us, but she also had a firm grasp of current events. The whole family assembled for the funeral at North Aston church and Timothy, by now ordained and a curate at Tunbridge, took the service.

In the flat, I used to hobble between bath and loo without shoes or caliper splint. Pooh stayed with me one night when my mother was at The Fox for a meeting and, as we rounded the corner from the loo, I caught my toe in the carpet and fell to the floor with such speed that nothing she did could save me. Both legs were bent up under me and my head and shoulders hit the wall. The first pain was excruciating in both legs and hip joints, but then it seemed to improve so I forbade Pooh to call a doctor, feeling that my chances of getting new employment would be even less with further health snags. Somehow Pooh shovelled me on to a low chair and from there into the bath; after a generous dram from the whisky bottle we managed to get me into bed, where I went thankfully to sleep. Although bruised and sore, next morning there were no obvious ill effects.

Out of work again, I contacted the local Disablement Resettlement Officer and was told that, as my pay had reached £1,000 per annum, I should have to be interviewed for the Professional & Executive Register. This sounded high-powered and I suggested it might be wrong for me, but my informant was adamant. The office where I was to be interviewed was in High Holborn and the first appointment they could offer me was ten days ahead. My mother and I set off there on a cold, blustery day and had great difficulty in securing a parking place. At last we found a meter from which there was a stiff uphill wheelchair push to the office building. We were ushered into moth-eaten surroundings and then into a room with a large desk at which was seated a sad-faced, laconic gentleman.

He asked what kind of work I had in mind. I boldly said I hoped for something in journalism, writing, publishing or even broadcasting. A bitter smile crossed the face of my interviewer as he told me that if any openings as interesting as that materialised, he and his colleagues would snap them up to escape from their own boring, underpaid jobs that had no future. Astounded by this outburst, I asked him if he had any employment suggestions suitable for me and he could do no more than shake his head with vigour. He then held forth for a whole hour, saying I must realise that my chances of employment were practically non-existent and that my most important task was to draw my social security. I had not come there for this advice and said so, for all he did was to emphasise the painfully obvious obstacles that had always faced me. I suggested that perhaps he had a more experienced colleague better able to deal with my complicated requirements.

'Oh no,' he replied with a sad smirk. 'You see, I am the overall head of this section and there is nobody who can tell you any more about anything here than I can.'

He had no suggestions either about training, and his performance in a period of so-called full-employment shocked me to the backbone. At least he promised to circulate my details to his colleagues in the London area, though he warned me that this was highly unlikely to help me. He saw us off and, as the lift gates were closing, adjured me again to remember to draw my social security benefit. We were met outside by a biting wind and when we reached our car there was a parking ticket stuck on the windscreen. This gave us the chance to vent our spleen in a letter to the police which resulted in the subsequent withdrawal of the summons on the grounds of extreme difficulty and provocation. That was something.

Long weeks followed with no news of jobs and I visited numerous private employment agencies to seek their help. While they did not manage to solve my problem, they were much more understanding and constructive than the 'specialists'. At last I was called for an interview, via the DRO, for an indexing and filing job that sounded well within my capacity. All hopeful, we attended at the address as arranged but on arrival were faced by a very tall front door step topped by a heavy swingdoor. Doggedly we procured the assistance of a passer-by to get me into the building, where we found two gentlemen obviously horrified by the extent of my disability – or actually by the fact that I was disabled at all. They kept shooting anxious glances at each other and shaking their heads frantically behind my back, where, misguidedly, they thought I could not see. Presumably they had not been warned about what was arriving and so got a nasty shock; therefore, their behaviour was hardly surprising. There was a faint gleam of relief in their eyes as they announced that the successful applicant must work on the first floor to which there was no lift. After that there was no more for me to say except 'good-bye', which left me feeling utterly rejected and useless.

I was slightly cheered to hear that the Principal of the House of Citizenship, Hartwell House, Aylesbury, was looking for a temporary tutor and would like to see me. Miss Dorothy Neville-Rolfe was the principal and as stories of her firm leadership had reached me in the past I now quivered with apprehension. The job of temporary tutor was combined with the duties of public relations officer, connected with the forthcoming visit of the Queen Mother; Her Majesty was to perform the ceremony re-opening a part of Hartwell House recently restored after the ravages of fire. When we got there Dorothy briskly ran through the work involved, over China tea and orange cake. She was not in the least bothered about my disablement. In fact, she told me that she had successfully accommodated disabled students so that if I chose to live at Hartwell she would be glad. I explained that the amount of care I required was such that I needed someone special to look after me, and was greatly relieved when she nevertheless declared that she was ready to appoint me on a part-time, non-residential basis. Owing to my lack of academic qualifications the pay was only £14 per week, but the therapeutic value of the work there did much to rescue me from the depression which had threatened to engulf me following my session with the High Holborn DRO.

Miss Neville-Rolfe made it clear that party politics were taboo at Hartwell, where lecturers were drawn from the widest variety of backgrounds and beliefs. The seventy girl students come from many nationalities and were mostly between the ages of sixteen and twenty-four, taking courses in arts and/or secretarial training. Having attended a staff meeting, I quaked to think of facing these sophisticated young ladies, armed with quantities of ‘O’ and, in some cases, ‘A’ levels. Nevertheless, my three months at Hartwell were full of colour and happiness. The people were delightful, the classes interesting and the weather fair. We would leave The Fox soon after dawn to be on duty at Hartwell by 8.45 a.m., and drove through countryside shrouded in early mists pierced by shafts of sunlight which spelled enchantment. The work was heavy. I had mounds of books to correct, speeches to tape, enquiries to answer, but the students and staff were unfailingly kind and helpful, in a way I had seldom known in a job during the past twenty years.

On the great day of the Queen Mother's visit it was arranged that, as a temporary member of staff, I should not line up with the others to be presented to Her Majesty, but would busily record the proceedings on tape behind the scenes. After the opening ceremony, the Royal party moved out into the garden and I was happily positioned at the back of the building, where I could watch. As they walked through groups of people stationed on the lawns, the Royal party suddenly veered round in my direction. In some agitation I hastily wheeled my chair backwards, but looked up to find that Her Majesty and Dorothy were gaining on me. About to accelerate backwards in case I was blocking their way to the cars, I suddenly spotted behind me a gaping coal-hole, so pulled up sharp. It was only then that I realised I had been their target all the time. Her Majesty had just returned from a hectic tour of Canada but showed no sign of fatigue when she very kindly spoke to me, saying that she knew her Secretary, Martin Gilliat, was a friend of mine. The general opinion was that the afternoon had gone extremely well. When the end of term arrived, both students and staff showered me with books and flowers, and Dorothy made several bookings for me to return to speak as an outside lecturer.

In an attempt to draw the attention of the Tories to the existing lack of provision for disabled people, I submitted, through the Wessex Area, a resolution for the National Party Conference asking for better social services for those who really needed them, and it was accepted for the agenda. The Conference was at Brighton and we were billeted in the party headquarters at The Metropole. I was due to speak at 9.30 a.m. on Friday, 15th October 1965, and a microphone was specially stationed where I could reach it. Speaking of the little known deprivations of long-term, severely handicapped people, I said that many were not eligible for financial provision and were not given the opportunity to work and earn money from home, so were unable to reward friends and relations who bore the burden of caring for them. While many families drawing family allowances and old age pensions could well do without them, the families I spoke of not only supported a severely disabled person but were further bludgeoned by real poverty. Lack of cash benefits and domiciliary help spelt for them a life of misery and despair. Mr Heath listened attentively and Keith Joseph and Edward du Cann appeared to take particular note of my remarks. The Resolution scored a triumph and got good press coverage, with generous reports in the *Daily Telegraph* and the *Yorkshire Post* and a reference in *The Times*. The *Brighton Argus* carried this headline in huge letters: 'Now a Tory plea for sick and old.' When I returned to London, Keith Joseph asked me to consider a document he was preparing on job opportunities for disabled people and I saw at once what a valuable and caring ally he was for all of us who were disabled.

We heard reports of two disabled housewives who had formed a group to high-light the pensionless plight of so many like them, and then a letter arrived inviting me to join their campaign. I tried hard to dodge them on the grounds that I was too busy with other commitments, for I was doubtful whether the cause of disability would be helped by launching a public attack about our impoverished situation. Our family code had been to try not to inflict our troubles on others. Finally, Megan Du Boisson got me on the telephone and, so as not to appear uncaring, I joined her Disablement Income Group – DIG for short.

For some years I had favoured the setting up of a form of 'roving almoner' system, in order to identify and care for handicapped people living in the community. I now wrote about it to the new M.P. for Barkston Ash, Michael Alison, who was one of the better and brighter people who had been working at CRD. He invited me to take a colleague who could also discuss the subject to lunch with him at the House of Commons. When Pix Hamilton could not accept, she suggested inviting Megan. My mother and I collected Megan from Waterloo Station and were surprised to see how mobile she was as she walked towards us, followed by a porter pushing a wheelchair which he placed in the boot of our car. We knew she suffered from multiple sclerosis and as this varies in intensity from day to day we were not unduly surprised by her mobility. Michael had kindly invited other M.P.s to meet us at lunch and Megan quickly made her cast iron points on the economic advantage to the whole community of making proper and fair provision for disabled people. Her facts were well marshalled and her crystal clear argument took wings to the extent that it was hard for anyone to intervene. The others seemed as impressed as I was by her performance, so the actual extent of her disability that day became unimportant.

A DIG branch was formed in Westminster and I attended the inaugural meeting. We were addressed by Mrs Lena Jager M.P. who asked if anyone there had found difficulties with steps blocking their way to work. Not naming my place of work, I said the steps at the front door had been a nightmare. Another lady said she had worked with NEDC at Millbank and every day had been faced by acres of steps to climb which, when wearing two caliper splints and using elbow crutches, had made things very hard. She turned out to be Mary Greaves, about whose daring exploits I had often been told. We were now both elected to the branch committee. DIG had several grudges against society, the main ones being that there was no financial reward for those who looked after severely disabled people living at home; that wives who became disabled and were insured on their husbands' cards had no claim for benefit; and that the so-called 'civilian' disabled were entitled to only a fraction of the benefit calculated as being fair for those who were disabled through industrial injury, even where the extent of handicap was the same. DIG told us of the total lack of provision for those people who had been too disabled to work to have enough stamps on their cards to be in benefit, and of the disincentive of the tax system whereby anyone who started to work again after being disabled could not earn more than £4 per week without losing the whole of his or her pension. The extra expense of disability was stressed – ranging from the heavy costs of special transport and the disadvantage of not being able to be a selective shopper, to the inability to do mending, decorating and minor household repairs – and DIG's pamphlets illustrated that people were too easily condemned to costly hospital beds when, if given the cash, they could live more happily and economically at home. It was shown that placing a disabled housewife in a residential establishment often entailed the break up of her family and the putting of her children into care.

Once again I called unsuccessfully on the DRO service. The private agencies, however, advised me to embark on a six-month course with the London School of Journalism. This gave me some sense of purpose. The pity was that I chose this moment to break my leg, slipping on black ice as my mother transferred me from car to wheelchair. At St Mary Abbott's Hospital they thought they would have to operate but, possibly because they found my breathing very bad, decided instead to keep the leg immobilised in bed. I had to stay the night there and was worried to find the nursing staff, kind and efficient as they were, somewhat dumbfounded at the extent of my paralysis. My breathing was so bad that I could barely tell them of the ephedrine drug I desperately needed to improve it. By the time I got my message across the pharmacy had closed, and I felt fairly close to dying several times that night. Next morning, with the required ephedrine, I was delighted to hear my mother declare that she chose to nurse me at home. The worst hurdle was to get me back to the flat, as the stretcher would not fit into our lift and the unhappy ambulance men were left to carry me up all of our five storeys. Things cheered up immediately we touched down and my mother proceeded to nurse me impeccably for the next seven weeks, backed up by an occasional visit from the district nurses. One little coloured nurse with poor English left this note for her colleagues: 'Mother cooping very well'. If it was 'coping' she meant, then she was absolutely right.

When I was better and had to draw my unemployment benefit, I was told to attend at the Brook Green Labour Exchange, Disablement section. To our exasperation we were faced again by the most enormous step. No pleadings on my part would persuade them to let me receive the pay by post, but at least those weeks strengthened my resolve to do what I could to get things improved.

We had various Conferences to attend and at Church House, Westminster, I was reminded that there was no accessible ladies loo. Our only hope was to shorthead the bishops into the door marked 'gents', which was nervous work for we never knew what we might find. Luckily neither they nor we got any ugly surprises.

Through a chance acquaintance, and my short course in journalism, I was given a part-time research and writing job on a free-lance basis with the Institute of Purchasing and Supply. My task was to compare copious lists of prices on the world commodity market in order to quote them in a weekly bulletin for which I wrote a 1,000 word commentary, compiled from sources spoken and written. I also contributed the leading article. My pay was £15 a week and the work took two and a half days. The only snag was that there were twelve most awkward steps to negotiate before reaching the lift to the office on the eighth floor. At least the steps were wide, so my mother got a garage to make two huge run-way ramps so that my chair could be pushed up by someone strong, but we needed bags of help with pushing, as well as with storing the ramps, which were clumsy and unwieldy. We made no fuss for the first two years and then a means was evolved by which I could work from home, so that either Prudence or a hired car ferried the documents between me and the office and I managed to get a small part of the expense involved paid by the Department of Employment. My copy had to be rushed to the office for the printers' dead-line at 3.30 p.m. on Thursday. It all worked out quite well for six and a half years.

After all the months I had spent searching for work, as soon as I got fixed up with the Institute, the Central Council for the Disabled asked if I would take on the post of appeals organiser. My pay with them would be £12 per week plus £400 to be claimed on expenses. Suddenly, my monetary situation was transformed, but there were accessibility problems still to be overcome. It may seem ludicrous, but the Central Council for the Disabled had a very off-putting flight of front door steps. On meeting days a ramp was fixed over the steps, but on other days I had to work at home.

At the 1966 Tory Conference at Blackpool I said that, having been unemployed and despairing when I spoke in 1965, I was now working and my outlook as a result was totally different. My message was that disabled people desperately needed better work opportunities. Because these remarks came from the heart they were well received, particularly by Mr and Mrs Iain Macleod. They sought me out and congratulated me for having illuminated a dimension of life that was not understood by everyone.

Now that I had a work schedule to govern my week, life became more agreeable. It became better still when Pooh decided to sell The Fox and take a flat on the first floor of Marlborough Court. Many nephews and nieces were by now married – Joan's Timothy, Jimmy's Martin, Edward and Jenny; Pooh's Maria – and only Robin remained. Unhappily, Maria's marriage had broken up and as Pooh's flat was bigger than she wanted, Maria moved in there, together with her dog and stacks of belongings. Having trained as both a secretary and as a cook, she undertook a number of cooking engagements before sailing to Australia and New Zealand where she stayed for some weeks with our faithful Bethell cousins.

At this time my hands started to go numb, so my doctor sent me to the National Hospital for Nervous Diseases, in Queen Square, for investigation. I spent a very unhappy few days there having a myelogram X-ray. The method was to inject ink into the spinal column and then tip the patient up and down while face down on a plinth, so that the course of the ink was carefully photographed and recorded. It was described to me beforehand as resembling a fairground ride, and certainly the plinth moved very fiercely both backwards and forwards as well as up and down; the radiation area meant that staff could not stand by to prevent me falling and although they had tried to tie me on, because my helpless arms and legs could not be secured properly, my limbs kept falling off and almost getting into the moving works. My breathing was laboured while I was on my face, and it was not possible to tell the experts about these horrors, especially while they were engrossed in their photography. The very high-powered radiologist explained before we started that he was using a new machine, which would be like driving a new and powerful car. I said I hoped he would not drive me into a ditch, at which point he gave me a lumbar puncture which rendered me incapable of further comment. After an hour of mental and physical torture, it was revealed that two displaced discs were sitting on a nerve in my neck and causing the numb hands. When I was told that they intended to go through the whole business again with me face upwards, I flatly refused to allow it. They had found the trouble so surely a further performance was not justified, especially as the lumber puncture had left me with an attack of lumbago. They prescribed a collar, which I wore for a year, but unluckily without any improvement. Luckily my hands have grown very little worse in the twelve or so years since that horrible outing.

We decided that driving from my neck, and parking in particular, was mainly responsible for the damage to my arms and hands, so I gave up driving. I heard of a mini-van adapted to accommodate a wheelchair, with an easy ramp to let down behind and an extra row of windows round the raised roof, providing a splendid view. It took two years to get this model, after finding all the details from the Disabled Living Foundation, but it was less heavy work for my helper than transferring me into a car and lifting my chair into the boot. Wherever we went our van caused a stir – some people laughed, but most applauded and asked for details of where to get it. Some said it was like 'Ironside' and others like a horsebox!

When we had to retire from the committee, the Nuffield Orthopaedic Centre gave us a splendid leaving party and Matron presented us with Hospital badges denoting length of service, which we were proud to wear. There had been a good family spirit amongst Committee members and staff which I am sure was to the benefit of patients. After more than forty-five years on hospital committees, my mother received the MBE in the 1967 New Year's Honours List. Pooh and I accompanied her to the investiture ceremony and were struck by the helpfulness shown towards my wheelchair. I was wheeled by a footman, who escorted me in the lift. That day, Her Majesty had a chill, so the ceremony was performed by the Duke of Kent, hurriedly summoned from Camberley. As an example of how thoughtfully he carried out his duties, from the several hundred who received awards that day he identified my mother and asked if she belonged to the Lane Fox family he knew in Yorkshire.

My begging work for the Central Council increased and I spent two days sorting through dusty old files at the Charity Commissioners, searching for trusts likely to contribute to our funds. My mother helped me with countless letters and set up a filing system in our flat – in fact, she did all the vital dogsbodying. Pooh got elected unexpectedly to a ward of the Royal Borough of Kensington & Chelsea, in North Kensington, which kept her fully occupied. Eventually, my appeal for the Central Council reached £12,400 in a little over two and a half years, in gifts and covenants, and, by introducing Ian Fairbairn to Lady Hamilton, we secured a further £8,000 from the Charitable Trust set up in memory of Esmée, given for the purpose of a campaign on accessibility. I was very happy about this result and therefore not a little surprised when a new director was appointed, to hear that he would make his own fund-raising plans and no longer required me – all the more mysterious when I received flowery letters of appreciation from the Chairman and Hon. Treasurer, asking me to keep in close contact with them.

8

London Becomes Me

Many disabled people of all kinds attended DIG's impressive Trafalgar Square Rally in 1966. It was addressed by Members of Parliament, clerics, the late Michael Flanders, and by Megan Du Boisson. Afterwards, we all trooped off down Whitehall to Downing Street, where Megan handed in a petition to No. 10. It sought a national disability income based on the extent of handicap and stressed the injustice suffered by the disabled housewife who was then excluded from receiving any invalidity benefit.

The Committee of our Central London (Westminster) branch was a motley crew and met each month in the flat of Dame Joan Vickers (now the Baroness Vickers) in Westminster Gardens. Despite our tedious discussions we were refreshed by pretty surroundings. Mary Greaves soon made it clear that she believed in activity and, as funds were short, nudged me into organising a DIG auction of books signed by their authors. First, I had to collect the books. My pleading letters brought forth works from authors ranging from J.B. Priestley to Enoch Powell, and no fewer than four members of the Birkenhead family generously donated editions – Freddy sent two. The other 100 writers included Harold Macmillan, Iain Macleod, Antonia Fraser, Kenneth Clarke, Roy Jenkins, Airey Neave, Aidan Crawley and Doris Leslie. I was especially glad to have two children's books by Hester. We housed the volumes under our beds and all over the flat, finding it difficult not to settle down in a corner to read them. We charged friends and acquaintances £2 a head for the privilege of coming to Dame Joan's flat, where we gave them a snack and a glass of wine and encouraged them to bid. Our success depended on having a knowledgeable and persuasive auctioneer. We were terribly lucky, and the skill of the auctioneer, together with the co-operation of our guests, resulted in a £400 profit.

Next morning, our smug satisfaction with this total quickly evaporated with the arrival of the hideous news that the auctioneer's gavel had left deep circles on the poor Dame's mahogany dining-room table. She was magnanimity itself in the face of our dumbstruck horror and even invited my mother and me to stay with her in her Plymouth constituency. We drove down – an adventure in itself – and found she had arranged a splendid programme for us, including visits to the many centres for disabled people with which she was connected. She had fixed up a ground floor bedroom for me, entertained us lavishly and even took us on a tour of north Cornwall.

We were all gathered in London for DIG's AGM when we received the horrific news that Megan Du Boisson had been killed in a road accident while on her way from Surrey to the meeting. Many of her devoted followers and allies were present, and the chairman, who was himself very upset, had to announce the tragedy to the meeting. It was unanimously agreed that she would have wished us to carry on with the meeting and, furthermore, that Mary Greaves should succeed Megan, an excellent choice. Our branch committee felt the loss of Mary's membership badly and there and then decided to split into two, one half making me its chairman. There followed three years of monthly committee meetings in our flat. One rewarding spin-off was that Jane Parkinson (daughter of Dorothy and Kenneth and now married to Simon Scrope) became a committee member. This was especially valuable as she was working in the Whips' office of the House of Lords. My nieces, Maria and Jenny, each did a stint as Hon. Secretary to our DIG committee. We worked very hard on fund-raising events, held in The King's Road Chenil Galleries, where we sold old clothes and other items from early morn to dusk, with good effect.

Such successes must have inspired DIG's Executive to make me chairman of its national fund-raising committee, which was both a challenge and a chore. Sometimes meetings were held in the House of Commons, sponsored there by one of the three Vice Chairmen who were M.P.s. As we passed along the corridors of power I would meet friendly Tory M.P.s who threw their arms round me as an old campaigner. As a result, DIG's left-wing began to consider me 'suspect'.

Amongst the many disabled people I was getting to know there now emerged a new breed who were both angry and aggressive. Some had welcome energy and application, but others (often the less severely disabled) were rather unreasonable in their demands. They seemed to want to use disablement as a means of changing the world by bloodless revolution. In my desire to be involved in making all aspects of our requirements clearly and fairly known I jumped at the chance to accompany Mary Greaves to a meeting in the House of Commons of the All-Party Parliamentary Group on Disability. I met there Socialist M.P.s Alfred Morris and Jack Ashley, together with old friends like Neil Marten and David Price. The meeting coincided with the passage of Alfred Morris' Chronically Sick and Disabled Persons' Bill, which, miraculously, he navigated through eleven government departments just in time to get it firmly on the Statute Book before the General Election of 1970. The idea was popular and had all-party support, for Jim Prior had had a somewhat similar Private Member's Bill turned down by the Labour Government, on the grounds that its provisions would be cared for in the forthcoming National Health Insurance Bill – a Bill which, in fact, never saw the light of day! The evening Jim Prior's Bill was debated, I was interviewed with him on BBC 2 and said then how bitterly I resented this delay to improve conditions by an apparently uncaring Government. Some months later, Alf Morris succeeded with his Bill; he richly deserved this crowning success to his skill and untiring efforts. I spent exciting hours in both Houses listening to the ensuing debates and through Jane's introductions, was enabled to sit as an observer on Lord Longford's committee which considered the Bill in the Lords.

This new Parliamentary awareness of our plight made me rub my eyes. It was all so different from the old familiar lack of understanding displayed at almost every level amongst nearly all able-bodied people, unless they had someone handicapped in their family. Our plight was now appreciated and catered for as never before – even local authorities seemed prepared to set aside cash to help us. Under the new 1970 Conservative Government, in which Keith Joseph was Secretary of State for Social Services, the first provision on the Statute Book was the introduction of the Attendance Allowance. This won approval from both parties and meant that for the first time many disabled people got an allowance with which to pay those deserving people who cared for them. My mother now received a tiny reward for the immeasurable help she gave me. As she had saved the State the cost of keeping me in residential accommodation for forty years, this seemed only fair. At last some injustices were being addressed.

I was tied up with work for the Institute that year and could not get away for a holiday until November, when Jimmy generously subscribed to our week at the Imperial Hotel, Torquay. My mother drove me down. A strong gust of wind caught the top of our little van on Salisbury Plain and we all but blew away. No doubt owing to the long drive, my mother woke up next morning with dreadful cramp in both legs. There was nobody else who could mobilise me, so she somehow managed to drag herself out of bed and crawl down the hill to a tobacconist, where she purchased a stout walking-stick. She returned leaning heavily on her new acquisition and referred no more to her indisposition, but the walking-stick has been her constant companion ever since. When we went the next year to Harrogate for York Races we took Pooh as our driver. On that Yorkshire trip Monna arranged for me to address the Leeds branch of DIG, which she had helped to inaugurate.

I joined a delegation to Keith Joseph at the Department of Health and Social Services and, while one or two of my DIG colleagues were opposed to him politically, all had to agree that he listened to our case with avid interest and even offered to address DIG's next big gathering six months ahead. As we left, he asked me if I was still doing the job with the Institute and I proudly answered that I was, feeling astounded that he should have remembered. The same delegation went the next week to the Shadow Minister for Social Services, Mrs Shirley Williams, who also received us well and appeared impressed by our case. These events made useful copy for me as the main contributor to DIG's Central London bulletin and writer of a regular page in the organisation's quarterly magazine *Progress*.

My clothes were always a bit of a problem, both to get and to maintain, and my mother put valiant effort into this. We raked stores and shops, creating chaos while she pulled me in and out of garments, for there appeared to be no alternative. The situation changed one Whit-Monday. I had failed to get the batteries of my chair charged up and wanted to use it over the holiday but found our garage closed, so we enquired around the street if anyone knew where we could find a charging-board. Behind me, I heard an oriental female voice say: 'You clome wid me, see my hosban', he help.' I smiled and tried to explain that she probably did not understand what we wanted, but she was insistent that we go with her. Mr Earp – for that was their name – turned out to be the English head chauffeur at the Thailand Embassy and my chair was fully charged by the next day. Mrs Earp followed me out to say she would like to do 'little bit dressmake' for me, and for the next eleven years, until her death, she largely solved my clothes problem.

Until she reached eighty, my mother firmly rejected all forms of daily help in London, but at last she agreed to have someone provided they came through the Kensington Social Services Department. The first lady decided to return to Ireland soon after she was engaged. The Department then announced that they had nobody to suggest except 'a gentleman', and they did not think we should like that. We asked them to send him along, half expecting to see some broken down old fellow. The front door bell rang at the appointed time and we were amazed to find, standing in the doorway, a tall and extremely good-looking young man – blonde, twenty-eight years-old, six feet three inches tall and with a soft American voice. He said he was afraid we should be surprised because we were probably expecting a lady I wanted to tell him we *were* surprised, but *not* for those reasons! His name was David Ford.

We looked forward to David's weekly visits with growing anticipation and he undertook all kinds of mammoth cleaning tasks. Stealthily we engaged him in conversation, discovering gradually that he had opted out of the rat race in New York to come and live in this country, and was now sharing a house with an actor playing on the West End stage. I pounced on any morsel of stage talk and also discovered that he had set aside his American qualifications and degrees in economics to take up social work. At DIG's next Wine and Cheese party at the Chenil Galleries David Ford took charge of the tombola. He became a leading helper as well as a valued and lasting friend.

Edward du Cann M.P. led a team in a 'My Witness' programme on BBC TV in debate with one led by Richard Taverne on the subject of whether the high rate of taxation was harming the country. DIG was asked to provide a spokesman for Edward. On the understanding that the views I expressed would be my own and not necessarily those of DIG, I agreed to take part. A studio audience acted as judges, and elaborate measures were taken beforehand to keep the identities of the team members secret. Our secret star was Sir Paul Chambers; we did not know till later that theirs was Sir George Woodcock. We won the toss and each team member was let into the central arena, around which sat the audience, feeling rather like the bull at a bullfight. We were faced by an amiable matador who gently waved the red cloak, in verbal form, to get us going. When Edward du Cann finished his questions he sat down, which was the signal for us to retire. As I was the last witness on our side, I watched the monitor until the person arrived who was to wheel me in. Edward asked where I lived and whether it was with my family, then sat down. At this point I broke all the rules in orders to declare that if my parents had not made sacrifices, personal and financial, I should have been committed to residential accommodation for the last forty years, yet that I doubted whether with today's high taxation any family now could do what they had done. Outside again, our team was told to go to the 'green-room' to watch the rest of the contest on a television monitor, so we raced down miles of corridors, through many swingdoors and up and down lifts, only to find when we got there the door firmly locked! Messengers scampered off to get keys and returned empty-handed. Luckily, we had a rugger-playing Welshman on our team who successfully charged the door with his shoulder. He broke the lock and let us in, just in time to hear that we had been declared the winners by one vote! Afterwards, both sides mingled amicably over drinks but, as we left, the contest was carried rather too far by one of our opponents who preceded us, flagrantly slamming every door shut in our faces.

My next sortie to BBC Television Centre was to represent DIG on a late-night programme with Alfred Morris, presented by Joan Bakewell, on the subject of the Chronically Sick & Disabled Persons' Act. My chief role was to complain that the disabled housewife was still without a pension.

Jimmy and Anne's son, Robin, never failed to win high academic awards during his school and University career, so it was no surprise to hear he was writing a book on Alexander the Great. He also supplied the *Financial Times* with weekly articles on gardening. While on holiday in Crete he lost the address of the friends with whom he was going to stay, together with all his money. At that point he chose to go to sleep by the side of the road. Shortly afterwards a car passed carrying his English acquaintances and somebody spotted him, woke him up and took him on board. The only passenger who did not know him was a girl called Louisa Farrell, to whom he very soon became engaged.

Most of the other nephews and nieces were married in London, always with Timothy officiating in some capacity. When Timothy got married to Mally, we toured up to Durham in mid-winter. Now we all went to Robin's wedding in Magdalen College, Oxford. The congregation in the College Chapel was a mixture of funny old dons, many Loyds and more Lane Foxes, Louisa's beautiful Paget aunts, plus her fabulous great aunt, Lady Diana Duff-Cooper. The church was decorated with sheaves of wonderfully fragrant lilies and it may well have been their fragrance that was to blame for one of my worst attacks of asthma. As I gasped at the reception kind people did their best for me, but inhaler, pills, soft drinks and hard drinks, were all to no avail. I only began to recover when we got away from the unfamiliar country air, which made me realise how hideously, but happily, urbanised I had now become.

Jimmy had successfully established a firm of estate agents called Lane Fox and Partners. As he had suffered a severe coronary attack, his sons, Martin and Edward, took a leading part from the beginning and it soon became a flourishing concern. Both have delightful families and have embarked on ambitious establishments, apparently without worrying about how to get people to help them, but certainly to the outsider their houses are well-run, comfortable and charming. They and Jimmy all have swimming-pools and I think wistfully how well we could have made use of one for my treatment with Monna. Jimmy used his for exercise after his coronary, from which he appears to have made a good recovery, although his formerly active routine has had to be exchanged for a more stay-at-home life style. Timothy was in Durham St John's Theological College, part of the university, where he lived happily with his wife and two children, but moved to the Parish of Darley Dale in Derbyshire; he is now styled the Revd Dr T.E. Yates.

A splendid concert was arranged by the Disabled Living Foundation at which those great pianists, Cyril Smith and his wife Phyllis Sellick, played three handed, proving how Cyril had cast aside the effects of a stroke. The compère was Michael Flanders. As Princess Alexandra was to be present and as the hall is reached by a formidable flight of stairs, we were asked to arrive early and enter via the kitchen lift. Half way through the performance I found it very hard to breathe, despite repeated applications of all the remedies I now never failed to carry. We beat a hurried retreat through the kitchen where I was by then in such trouble that I could not even thank my carriers and helpers. Once home, however, things appeared to return to normal again.

In 1972, Central London DIG decided to raise funds by singing carols on Victoria Station, so my mother and I went as collectors. Travellers were surprisingly generous, but the contributor I remember the most clearly had a very red face which he stuck right into mine, saying as he did so: 'Do you ever get the 'flu?' The point of his remark was lost on me, until I was laid low by a high temperature a few days later. My mother and Pooh nursed me in the flat with an occasional night nurse for fourteen days, which included Christmas day, during which time my doctor tried numerous antibiotics without success. Apart from a fleeting doze, sleep was beyond me and the experience was like a diabolical nightmare, my face, eyes, mouth and throat so swollen up from allergies that I could neither eat nor drink and could barely speak. My doctor became alarmed and summoned a consultant from St Thomas's Hospital, who ordered me to be collected at once by ambulance and admitted. The ambulance kept us waiting for three and a half hours. By the time we were on our way I was almost delirious, convinced we were driving through an air battle at the height of the blitz.

I am a staunch admirer of St Thomas's and doubt if there could be a better hospital in the world. Nevertheless, I found that even in such dedicated and superb surroundings minor horrors can occur. When we reached Florence Ward we found the Sister was on leave. My mother and Pooh were, however, quite impressed, and left feeling I would be adequately cared for. A staff nurse wheeled a cylinder of oxygen towards me, tried it, and couldn't make it work. With a colleague she made a few hasty repairs, then said to me rather crossly: 'Well, I hope this will be all right *now*!' She thrust into my hand a mask, which was something I had never seen before. Looking sternly at me and ignoring my disorientated state, she said: 'You must hold this on your face, but you have to take it off if you have something to cough up, when you must use this carton.' She held out what looked like an empty ice cream carton. Because I could not speak properly it was impossible to say that, in this recumbent position, my hands would hardly work at all, and certainly could not do all that. She left and I felt totally alone. I tried unsuccessfully to follow the instructions and just hoped the nurse might see my difficulties. When her colleague arrived, it was to pour a hot drink into my raw mouth, which caused me excruciating pain. I wept miserably and the staff began to look at me with quizzical glances. When the lady medical registrar arrived by my bedside I was virtually past caring – until she drove a needle into an artery which really hurt. Feeling ill-used and angry, in sign language I asked for the telephone, wanting desperately to make sure that at least the others had got home safely, irrespective of how I was coping. They left the telephone beside me, but I could not possibly reach the receiver and had nothing to put in the coinbox to pay for the call and with nobody there to help me, the telephone seemed to jeer at me.

My nightmares became ceaseless, night and day. One involved members of DIG who seemed to tie me to a stake and train on me their bows and arrows, saying I had let them down and this was their revenge. Then came a counter-attack by my family who ran the gauntlet of fierce hospital defences under supporting air cover, led by my consultant. The next day they told me on the medical round that whether I would recover depended on the amount of effort I made with the physiotherapists who would come to beat me. As I was too exhausted to utter a sound, I did not ask them for further explanation. When the physiotherapists arrived, the poor things were rather appalled to find a dead lump paraplegic needing to be treated for respiratory troubles, which meant moving the lump about a lot. In these circumstances they found me both hard to handle and still more difficult to understand.

For many days it seemed to me that a procession of people in white coats stopped just long enough by my bedside to stick a needle into me and retrieve blood, which often had to be arterial and proved painful to remove. There was a shortage of bedside nursing and nobody stayed long enough to give me time to try and tell them what I was up against. One day I felt much worse and they gave me enormous injections, after which persons and events became cloudy. My day and night dreams persisted, with graphic pictures of members of my family; my mother especially appeared to be mercilessly grilled, then edged towards extermination. A small packet of self-raising flour appeared frequently, and when I started to get slightly better that packet began to wink at me, before revealing that what it really contained was my mother and not flour at all. She was victorious from that point and my recovery began then.

My home suppliers quickly started to provide all the bland delicacies, such as banana squash, that would not hurt my mouth. Then wonderful champagne began to arrive from Jimmy and from Kenneth Parkinson, so life gradually grew much better.

Pooh was asked to bring my clothes and help to dress me; we put on my dressing-gown and caliper splint, with shoes, and attempted to get me transferred to my wheelchair. What we had not allowed for was the slippery floor, and no sooner had my foot touched the lino than it shot out under the bed, leaving Pooh and her helpers hanging gallantly on until urgently summoned porters appeared.

Because I had become emaciated, my elbows and heels got sore easily and I asked for sheepskin to protect them. It proved curiously hard to get until, on one of her many visits, my mother suggested she would bring some from home, after which announcement hospital supplies became available whenever required. By then I was well enough to notice other patients and began to realise that some were extremely ill. Visitors to a newcomer on my left told me that although she was not expected to live long after having suffered an extended illness, the chief pain which she now endured was caused by sore heels. They wanted sheepskin for her but had so far failed to get any. I rashly promised that when I was discharged she should have mine, and hate now to recall that in the fuss and confusion of leaving I failed her. When I got home and telephoned the charge nurse, I got a fairly frosty answer. Communications were not their strong suit, a fact illustrated by the answer my mother received from the ward desk to her enquiry about me: ‘Oh, she’s all right. Just very wandery, but then I expect she always is!’ My mother was not amused – and when she told me some months later, neither was I.

Before I was discharged, someone called Dr Spencer came to see me, as a friend of Lady Hamilton’s. It appeared that he belonged to St Thomas’s but was also in charge of another hospital dedicated to bad respiratory cases. I was not in favour of the ‘establishment lot' and noted, with relief, that this man did not fit into that category. He had a healthy, outdoor appearance and even his white coat looked more of the kennel, than of the clinical, variety. He told me that from what he heard of my everyday breathing troubles, these must now be treated seriously to prevent my running into the same kind of trouble again. He explained that I had become disorientated this time from a shortage of oxygen through a weakness caused by polio, so on hearing that, I was only too ready to fall in with any of his suggestions. He asked me to go for two or three nights to the respiratory unit he ran for St Thomas's at the South-Western Hospital in Stockwell, as soon as I had recovered from this experience. This clearly was the sensible course and his conversation made me realise that I must now attend to my longstanding respiratory troubles, which up to now I had managed to shrug off. This aspect of my health had to be faced even if it made giving up the more taxing of my work commitments, which I treasured so much. So after six and a half years I ceased to work for the Institute of Purchasing & Supply but at least it was good to tender my resignation this time, rather than find myself made redundant.

We discovered the South-Western Hospital, situated between Clapham and Brixton, approached by a fairly unsalubrious thoroughfare. We were instructed to enter Phipps Ward, but saw no way of doing so until a builder's labourer came to our rescue. When at last we got inside we were first struck by the array of iron lungs and other equipment and then by the wonderfully relaxed atmosphere. The Sisters-in-charge were in a strange state that day, one being in a wheelchair with a damaged ankle and the other still mobile but about to have a baby. They were both very nice. The ward is halved by the main hospital corridor, with the Sisters' office in the west end and the kitchen in the east end.

To lift me on to a high hospital bed, help was obtained from a white coated gentleman called Frank Kelly and it quickly became obvious that the staff really did know how to cope. They tried hard to teach me to frog breathe and although my instructress left me in no doubt that this was a lifeline which could save me in the future, despite rigorous practise I failed her lamentably.

I felt like the new girl at school amongst the other patients who were familiar with the ward and for the most part needed more help than I did. Some were very unmobile and amongst these was a very attractive and amusing girl called Susan. She had an acute brain and sharp sense of humour; her command of the situation left me feeling the size of a pigmy. She had a faithful ally called Victor, a good-looking young man with long legs but whose torso was badly misshapen from a sequence of operations when he was a child, carried out to try and improve his shoulders and arms. His head was now permanently turned over his left shoulder and the whole situation was made worse for him by his dreadful respiratory troubles. He needed to sleep in a respirator (of the kind I still called the iron lung until I quickly learnt to call it a tank) and required help to dress and undress. Once up, he strode along with an authoratitive air, as he left to spend his working day at a highpowered job in electronics. Amongst the others there was Tony, a fine young man permanently immobilised on a long chair but who had painted some arresting landscapes.

The doctors warned me that they wanted to test my blood gases to ensure there was not too much carbon dioxide present, and that to get a true reading they must take arterial blood while I was asleep during the night. I am always a light sleeper so I awoke at 3.30 a.m. to find a doctor and nurse stealthily loosening my bedclothes. They had warned me that if I was not asleep they would have to do this performance all over again, so now I feigned sleep and swallowed my groans as the needle hit a nerve. At least they got their blood sample.

The 'lingo' on the ward was new to me. Patients asked each other about their 'vital capacity', which sounded a bit near the knuckle until it was revealed that the phrase referred to the measure of their ability to inhale and exhale. They asked if you could frog breath, if you used a tank, curass or pump, if you had been put on a rocking-bed, or if at any time you had had a tracheotomy and been attached to a respirator. To date, I had got by on my old inhaler topped up by ephedrine pills, though there had been anxious moments lately, both at the concert and the wedding. Suddenly I started to get appalling attacks of asthma in hospital, so my blood gases were taken and found to be bad. Lung X-rays showed nothing at all extraordinary, though as a result of my pneumonia attacks there was residuary damage to account for these alarming moments of respiratory failure. Physiotherapy twice a day was ordered and I was put on a rocking bed, then persuaded to change my old inhaler and ephedrine for more suitable medications.

At first I hung perilously between one attack and the next and there seemed small hope of encouraging my vital capacity to rise from the 400–700 mark to the tolerated 1,500–2,000 'blow'. My mother was allowed to stay in the accommodation used for helpers of badly handicapped people in the nurses' home. Each morning she arrived at breakfast time, longing to hear that I had slept better, only to be told that I had constantly woken up feeling practically unable to breathe. Time after time the night staff came to my rescue, and summoned the physiotherapist who then wheeled in a magnificent piece of life-saving machinery called a Bennett respirator. The doctor also had to be got out of bed, so it was lucky that he was an extremely considerate and intelligent young man who never seemed to resent these calls. When all else had failed to get me back into reasonable health, they resorted to steroids, very cautiously and watching for side-effects all the time. The improvement in my days and nights was amazing, although I still panicked and wondered if I would ever be weaned away from hospital. I even dreaded any mention of the subject. It seemed incredible when Dr Spence announced that a smaller edition of the Bennett respirator, in which I had such trust, was now on the market and might be the right equipment for me at home.

Each day at the hospital I was busily working out and typing appeal letters on behalf of DIG. Now my mother insisted that, as I was away from St Thomas's, I must write to the Governors to tell them about the hazardous and slippery floors on Florence Ward, and about the difficulty in getting sheepskin. So when I heard that the Governors were going to pay a visit to Phipps Ward, I shook with apprehension. How stupid this was! When they arrived they told me they were grateful to have honest and outspoken comment. This was a huge relief to me and emphasised what a fine hospital St Thomas's is.

News reached me on the grapevine that Sir Keith Joseph, Secretary of State for Social Services, was due to visit the hospital and the unit. On the appointed day it was important for all to operate the specialist equipment and apparatus prescribed for our various requirements. I was put on the rocking-bed, with which I was very familiar, and sundry other patients displayed much more demanding contraptions; there were also the ambulant who, despite immense disabilities, undertook important work and needed to preserve their breathing – like Roy, a senior lecturer at Surrey University. As Keith Joseph rounded the corner of my cubicle he at once recognised me and looked amazed to see me bouncing up and down on a rocking-bed. He engaged me in a long conversation, so the photographers closed in and got good shots of us both, looking not a little surprised at our very mobile surroundings.

The last thing Keith Joseph expected was to see me three days later when, true to his promise, he addressed the DIG AGM at Imperial College. The hospital had allowed me to go, provided I took with me my new Bennett respirator and got it plugged into the mains there. Evidently I looked as peculiar as I felt since this was my very first outing; everyone recoiled aghast when they saw me but then were extra kind and benevolent. As we arrived, the chairman announced that I had been elected to the management committee, so we had to arrange for me to be lifted on to the platform which was eight and a half feet high. Luckily for me, the BBC Panorama team was present for filming and when they saw that the steps were too narrow to take my chair, they volunteered to carry me straight off the floor in my wheelchair on to the stage and to set up the Bennett beside me. Keith Joseph's address was sound, sincere and compassionate; those DIG members who jeered and shrieked because he did not offer an immediate cash bonus made me feel sick with disapproval of such loutish behaviour, which I felt must harm our cause. Most of the noise came from people who were very slightly disabled or even able-bodied, who were just there to rock the political boat. I was saddened to think of all my generous friends and acquaintances whose arms I had persistently twisted to get DIG funds.

Once discharged from hospital I had to build a new kind of life, one which might spare me those grisly wheezing attacks. My bedroom was now equipped with my invaluable Bennett, together with an electrically controlled Bickerton bed to sit me up and lower me down at the touch of a button. My confidence in these machines was soon established, reinforced by the knowledge that skilled technicians from Phipps Ward would come out to repair them at a moment's notice. Everyone on the Ward is known by their first name and it was always a pleasure to see the technicians – Frank, John, Mick and co. – but never more so than when a machine went wrong. Having seen in hospital the success with which these characters could reassure the patients, I was intrigued to learn that Frank had discovered his art of helping people to face up to a situation, however hard, while in the hands of the Russians at the end of the war. A book was written and published about his horrific experiences which made it easier to appreciate how, when faced with an apprehensive patient on a life-support machine, he could communicate his extra dimension of understanding.

Without being unduly morbid, in the past I had wondered what I would do if I got ill, so it was now a huge relief to find this ward. It understood my case and did not expect me to be able freely to move my hands and arms about. In charge was an inspired and exceptional man, Geoffrey Spencer. He stood on no ceremony, spread a healthily positive attitude and encouraged patients to make the very most of their lives. There are those who might consider many of the cases little more than dustbin fodder, but if so I felt privileged to be one of them. The skill and care bestowed on us by Dr Spencer was moving to witness and gratifying to receive. Phipps Ward with its excellent Sisters Tierney and Luke, its first-class physiotherapy and nursing, had an atmosphere where openness was the key-word and staff really understood the patients. This compared well with another London hospital where, when as a nurse watched my mother undress me and remove my caliper splint, she mistook it for an artificial leg and registered me as an amputee. Her colleagues were later amazed to find I had two legs when they dressed me to go home. Phipps Ward was not like that. They were well used to dealing with people in extraordinary predicaments, dependent on all kinds of gadgets and equipment, but in no way would they jump to summary conclusions without checking – which seems only right and fair. Geoffrey Spencer was self-effacing to a fault and insisted that Phipps Ward's achievements were due to team work. In that team he included the cleaners, kitchen staff, all nursing staff, physiotherapists, technicians, medical social workers, porters, X-ray department personnel, medical staff and all the backing of St Thomas's. They certainly knew how to deliver the goods.

9

Getting it Together

Provided I remembered when to take my various medicaments it was marvellous to be home again. My breathing was better than it had been for ages and even allowed me to have an unbroken night instead of the four hours' sleep that had been my lot for some twenty years. My mother must have been thankful not to have my bell rung, for I used to get her to change my position in bed after spending long hours awake.

Now, every four or five weeks, I attended the hospital for blood gases to be checked and, despite the searing pain the tests caused, it was reassuring to have positive proof that I was not likely to 'go bonkers' again – at least, not just yet. My instructions were to be co-operative and go to hospital if my breathing became troublesome. When I did so they kept me in just long enough for the rocking-bed, physiotherapy and an adjusted pill routine to do the trick. A visiting consultant once suggested that it might be helpful if my pulse rate were checked regularly at home, if there was someone there who could do this. When the houseman suggested this could be done by my mother who was well over eighty, the consultant said, not unnaturally, that a woman of that age could not manage this properly. The houseman, however, stood up in furious defence of my mother, saying he could think of few people who would be more competent and reliable to take it on.

Already my mother had become a kind of fable with the nursing staff. They were astounded to find that she could move me about unaided, as, until hoists were later introduced for use in the ward, it took two porters to lift me on to the bed or into the chair, for – apart from the singular technique my mother had evolved – there was no other way to deal with me. Small wonder that on our return trips new members of staff were waiting to see this incredible matriarch, who was never known to whine about her own deafness or aches and pains, but just got on with whatever had to be done, at the same time leavening the task with her own dash, wit and style. The story went that while she was staying in the nurses' home she heard cries from a third floor bathroom where a nurse had got firmly locked in. After spirited consultations through the door, my mother announced her intention to clamber along the narrow ledge outside in order to pass a key in through the window. This perilous expedition had just commenced when, in desperation, the nurse used brute strength and managed to force the lock.

Gradually, over the months and years, I became less mobile. Eventually it terrified me to think that I might fall on my mother as she hauled me to my feet to transfer me from chair to bath, or bed or loo, for if I fell on her I should squash her flat. It became a very alarming exercise and she had to bully and drive me to get me going. My legs seemed incapable of following my instructions; moreover, my leg and thigh began to ache abominably every time I lay down, so that I tried to race the pain by getting off to sleep before it began. The fact that this was connected with my earlier falls never occurred to me, but on my next visit to hospital they X-rayed the area in question which revealed that my hip, thigh and pelvis were totally out of place, a fact which fully explained my worsened mobility. I was offered surgery, but

I felt that my standing days were numbered so there would be little point in that. My left foot had received the worst bludgeoning from the polio attack and began now to be increasingly sore and swollen. Each day my mother spent anything up to an hour trying to put the shoe on, padding and protecting my foot with felt, cotton wool and an elastic stocking. Even when apparently in order, it would sometimes play up and require the whole process to be done again. My mother does not claim to be naturally patient, so how on earth she bore this introduction to the day is quite beyond me. Whenever my foot was treated by a chiropodist – or even if it just heard the word – it objected frantically and became worse for days. It was hardly surprising that I longed to pacify this obnoxious appendage by not having to stand up nor wear a shoe at all.

Daylight began to glimmer when the Social Services Department of the Royal Borough of Kensington and Chelsea installed a Wessex electric hoist for the bath, though it was hard to use satisfactorily because the bathroom was so tiny. Soon afterwards, on Phipps Ward, I was introduced to a manually operated Ambulift hoist, and delighted when Dr Spencer decided I ought to have one for the flat; by now the Phipps team had won my confidence and I was in favour of them taking such decisions for me. The Ambulift operates on the fork lift system, so that when it has me dangling mid-air from its chains, supported by two slings, my mother shoves, hauls and wheels it to the required spot and then lowers me. This hoist is cumbersome and we use it in my carpeted bedroom when it should really run on lino, but it has many good points and quickly won our firm allegiance. When the hamstring muscles of my right leg became useless, our old standing routine to transfer became impossible, so the hoist, plus considerable subtlety and finesse, was needed to get us by.

As flat-owners, we became increasingly anxious about maintenance charges and high rates. I wanted to get more mechanical or other assistance for my mother in the flat, too. Having been on the Council's housing-list for five years, we now applied for special accommodation, favouring the Cheshire Homes Housing Estate at Tulse Hill, Streatham. We looked at the flats there and found advantages in accessibility, lifts and well-placed hoists. There was a resident warden for emergencies, and district nurses and home helps provided daily assistance. A flat with a good outlook was vacant, but it transpired that unless I had someone living with me who was younger than my mother, I would not be acceptable as a tenant. For our part, we were not too keen on the road outside, which was not completed, nor on the steepish slope that led to the shops. As those circumstances were clearly against us, I decided to try and introduce some of the advantages I had noted into our flat I started by ringing the Social Services Department. They were very helpful and constructive, agreeing with me that it would be happier and more economical for both parties if, instead of having to admit me to expensive residential accommodation, they were to adapt the kitchen and bathroom of my flat to make it easier to live in. Plans were swiftly drawn up to demolish the wall between loo and bathroom, thus making a greater area in which to operate the electric hoist in both directions. The door to the kitchen would be widened and equipment re-arranged. The Council's first move was to instal an electronically controlled front door opener, working on an intercom system from a microphone unit plugged in to any of the rooms. This proved to be a great success.

Had we not determined to keep calm we might have been demented by the delay of nearly two years which elapsed before the planned alterations began. During this time we experimented with the district nurses who called regularly to help with my bathing arrangements; we found them helpful and efficient, though there was no certainty as to what time they would call. They were astonished by my mother's capabilities; she was very different from their usual 'over-eighty' charges.

D-day for our kitchen was August 1976. We ignored broad hints to move out while the workmen were there, staying put instead as a daily reminder of their need to be speedy. The wall was soon demolished and sheets were hung over doors to my bedroom against the builders' dust, in spite of which I was on one occasion driven to take refuge in hospital. At one hideous point there was no water, and then Prudence's loo was much in demand; anyone who met my mother in the lift and suspected that under the huge pile of bathtowels she carried there lurked a bedpan would have been right.

The two workmen made themselves quite at home and stacked their oldest boots bags and tools in our bath. We refused to complain except about the most flagrant breaches of etiquette and this policy usually paid off, though in the process we lost our spare back door key. The key was handed over as an olive branch, intended to save my mother from either persistently having to open the door or having to live with it open. While the kitchen was virtually gutted, my mother conjured up morsels from I know not where, speeding through the kitchen with a sly biscuit, during which she found herself drawn into the frequent breaks for chat between the workmen. She was sometimes allowed to take part in their crossword puzzles and once was consulted on a four-letter clue described as 'swearword' – she was much relieved to hear that it started with 'd' and ended with 'n'.

The Wessex electric hoist was at last in position and worked well, whereas the 'closomat' loo had to await expert attention from Manchester before it could demonstrate its wonders. Although two washbasins were broken, the kitchen fared better and equipment was well placed; after the painter had finished it looked most impressive.

The Council's trainee architect had done us proud, so we consulted her about where to get linoleum for kitchen and bathroom. The manager of the lino firm told us when to expect his fitter but having learnt that time meant little to such people, we were not surprised when nobody arrived at the appointed time. Next day we heard a thunderous knock on the backdoor. My mother adopted her most engaging smile to greet this loud visitor and when he said: 'Your bloody lift is out of order!' she knew he must be the lino man. She was about to offer to help carry the roll of lino up the five floors, when I sped round the corner in my chair to add my welcome. One look at me and he wagged a furious finger and, with a venomous look in his eye, declared: 'You want showing what work's all about, you do!' On this note we parted company. Later we discovered that he had a heavy weight of home worries in the form of a French wife, six children and an ill-afforded yacht costing £50 a week to moor. Our own niggling worries were nothing compared with that, so we were glad to shut the door and settle down to tea. These six weeks with the workmen in residence were best forgotten, but though they proved unpredictable, often unreliable and always a law unto themselves, they were perfectly pleasant. The final result certainly was most satisfactory and we blessed the Council for making it possible.

Dr Spencer had prescribed the closomat loo, which quickly became a godsend: it both washed and dried, thus eliminating the need for loo-paper. Together with the hoist for bed and bath, our routine was now revolutionised. As the new equipment took some getting used to my mother or I sometimes pulled the wrong controlling string of the hoist, sending me zooming up and away where I did not want to go. Apart from this minor difficulty the new arrangement was a great success, especially combined with the re-vamped kitchen. Washing-up was my best kitchen activity and the different varieties of gadgets and detergents made the whole dreary business much easier than when I had last taken my place at the sink, at the age of twelve. Extra free-running drawers in our sink-unit were vital to me for putting things away, which is a managerial job I rather like.

John Schuster telephoned one evening from Oxfordshire. His old friend, 'Evelyn Sharp', was doing what he thought was a one-man survey into transport for disabled people, but I knew well she was preparing a report ordered by Keith Joseph and eagerly awaited by everyone in the field of disability. John asked to bring her to see me and in particular, my van as she was interested in the predicament of the disabled passenger. After her visit she wrote me a charming letter which forecast that this would not be the last time we should communicate. After a long and powerful career in the Civil Service, she was made a distinguished member of the House of Lords.

A great deal appeared in the press about the start of the independent local radio in London and I listened avidly. It soon became obvious that phone-in programmes could be useful for disseminating snippets of helpful information for disabled people. Going a step further, I used this means to carry on a late night conversation with knowledgeable presenters. For several nights the much publicised Fiona Richmond was a guest in the studio. It irritated me when she made mincemeat of every well-meaning caller who dared to disapprove of her 'free-love-for-all' philosophies. When I rang in, I praised her on the easy charm of her telephone sessions, adding that, while I did not question her morals and way of life, I was deeply concerned about health hazards. She assured me that she never failed to have regular hospital checks, to which I retorted that I really was not concerned about *her* health but was very anxious about that of the naive young girls who listened to the radio and might well decide to emulate her chosen life style. It was my view that advocating any way of life which could lead to venereal disease and add to the risk of greater numbers of handicapped children was no less than a criminal offence. She did not reply to my outburst but the presenter of the programme thanked me and treated me with more respect than most of her less fortunate detractors.

Nobody could have been more surprised than I to receive a letter from Lord Aylestone, Chairman of the Independent Broadcasting Authority, inviting me to serve on the IBA's local radio advisory committee for London. The committee was set up to give the Authority advice and information that would be appropriate 'for reflecting, so far as is reasonably practicable, the range of tastes and interests of persons residing' in the area. Similar committees were formed to cover each of the other eighteen Independent Local Radio Stations, the difference for London being that it had two – Capital and LBC – within its remit, while elsewhere each committee was concerned with only one. I was mystified as to who had nominated me for this appointment which appealed to me so much, but when I heard that Lady Sharp was a member of the IBA I felt sure she must have been responsible. I accepted eagerly and attended the first quarterly meeting at the IBA headquarters at 70, Brompton Road; gallant fellow members and IBA officers nearly ruptured themselves to carry me and my wheelchair up a short, sharp and very difficult flight of stairs to the dining-room, for the excellent lunch which preceded the meeting. Later, we mercifully discovered that, by taking a lift to the eighth floor and wheeling me around the roof, we could use another lift to get me down to the right room. Even in a snowstorm the view from the roof was panoramic, which added to the stimulation and excitement I found in being involved in this new and increasingly powerful method of communication within London.

While the stations were still drawing up their programme schedules, I wrote to suggest they should include short items useful for disabled listeners. No reply came from either company until months later, when DIG was arranging to hold another rally in Trafalgar Square. Capital Radio telephoned. They asked me to propose three people to accompany me and take part in a programme to be presented by Joan Bakewell. I collected up two bright boys from DIG's Executive Committee, both in wheelchairs, and David Price M.P., who was married to a beautiful and clever paraplegic. The programme was fun, lasted an hour and went out late at night. At 9.00 a.m. the next morning, LBC rang to ask if I would like to put out a short, weekly spot on disablement subjects, to be called 'News and Information for Disabled Listeners'. This was exactly what I wanted. An interview was fixed for Monday. In order to be there on time, we did a Sunday reccy to plot our route to LBC's headquarters, well concealed in Gough Square behind Fleet Street. We were told it was easiest to arrive on foot in order to dodge round the alleyways, but that was no good to us, so, following the signs to Dr Johnson's house, we at last found the charming little Boswellian square. Cars and motor bikes were active around a modern office block and I soon realised with inexpressible delight that not only was this our destination *but that it had no front door step*! I went home purring with happiness and slept soundly that night.

My mother and I arrived in good time on the morrow. She unshipped me and pushed me in the wheelchair inside the frontdoor, where we were confronted by the cruellest flight of nasty steps up to a lift. At ground level there was nothing but the commissionaire's office and a perilously twisting stair leading down to the basement studios. I found it hard not to burst into tears of desperate disappointment and then bolt for home, but someone thoughtfully sent a message to ask the panel to interview me where I was. At that point the man who was then IBC's Chief Editor, Marshall Stewart, came through the door. We had met at the IBA and I seized the opportunity to ask him what hope there would be of broadcasting my piece from my van parked outside? He was encouraging, and when the producer also agreed I commenced a stint of three years of weekly five-minute programmes recorded from my van parked in Gough Square. There we competed with the noise of taxis making U-turns, motor bikes revving up and rain dropping on our tin roof, not to mention the lady traffic wardens who thought they were going to make a killing until they discovered I was the proud holder of an orange badge, that blessed passport to easier mobility for disabled people. Despite the stairs, I was twice on air from the studios, carried down by marvellous presenters and producers who were prepared to risk their wind and limbs to get me there. After this I took a firm line with them, however, for I knew too much about slipped discs and ruptures to wish to cause them here.

Mark Elwes, a fellow member of the local radio advisory committee, spontaneously gave stalwart support in trying ingenious ideas to get me broadcasting opportunities. The actor, Jeremy Brett, indirectly helped him to get me on the BBC3 programme 'Woman of Action'. Jeremy had already been extremely hospitable by including my mother and me in wonderful parties at his house, planned with our 'home help' friend, David Ford. To get me into the house they had to carry me up a very tricky flight of steps. I met such fascinating individuals as Bamber and Christina Gascoigne, Penelope Keith and Johnnie Saunders at these parties, and all were very kind to us. Jeremy knew I was longing for more work opportunities and in order to provide Mark Elwes with a means of promoting my chances, taped a conversation we had together. Armed with this, Mark persuaded Derek Drescher, then producing 'Man of Action', to contact me. At first the challenge thrilled me to the marrow, but I was then daunted by the realisation that it meant collecting enough musical thought to fill eighty minutes, with very little chat and a lot of careful selection. The best plan seemed to be to outline the story of my life punctuated with favourite pieces of music. My choice of records included Nannie Holland's favourite on the nursery gramophone, 'The Red, Red Robin', Hutch's 'I Travel Alone' and Noel Harrison's 'The Windmills of the Mind'. Then we had Kathleen Ferrier's 'What is Life Without Thee', 'The Battle Hymn of the American Republic', to which I had become firmly attached when watching Sir Winston's funeral, and Noel Coward's 'That is the End of the News', not to mention snatches of Schubert, Debussy, Haydn, and pieces played by Dame Myra Hess, Cyril Smith and others.

We had to have something descriptive of the sea to represent my horrific time at Filey when I had contracted the crippling disease, but I had not quite bargained for Debussy's 'La Mer'. It seemed to last for hours.

We had sent post cards to such friends as we could alert to hear my programme and many of them, plus a few more, together with listeners who had just found me on the radio by chance, contacted me by telephone or post. Some listeners wrote who did not know me at all. The actual recording was a challenging ordeal. I sat, script in hand, waiting for the green light to show me when I was on air, conscious of the awkward names of musicians which I had to pronounce, while overlooked through a picture window by the producer and engineer. It was no sinecure. Nevertheless, the fat cheque I received left me feeling more than well rewarded for my endeavours.

Again through Mark's efforts, Thames Television announced that they wished to prepare a programme about my mother and me. They hoped to hear about my background and my views on present provision for disabled people. I was still deeply immersed in this when a large envelope arrived from the Prime Minister's Office to ask if I had any objection to receiving the OBE. Of course, I did not refuse, and privately noted that it was a wonderful bit of direction by the Almighty to deal me this card just now. The New Year could not arrive quickly enough because I detest having to keep secrets. As usual, Paul Stobart stayed with Pooh for Christmas and we played our traditionally wild games of Bridge, which kept my mind off the forthcoming announcement. When the New Year at last arrived I could not at first find myself in *The Times*' honours list, for I was posted as: 'Miss F.L. Fox, for work with disabled people'. The *Yorkshire Post* loyally published a terrible photograph of me, and the *Oxford Mail* gave my award a special mention. LBC sent a reporter to interview me, and from then on the news began to trickle through, bringing a rush of heartwarming letters. They meant a lot.

Martin Gilliat arranged to celebrate the event with dinner for eight of us at Bucks Club. Hester came all the way from Wantage; the company was excellent and the dinner delicious. On arrival, my mother and I were keen to navigate the Club steps without alerting anyone, but she got caught up in parking the van and

Martin and a porter were too quick for us. They very kindly took over the chair before I had time to explain that certain adjustments had been made to it, with the result that I was all but tipped out on my face at the feet of two people alighting elegantly from a taxi, before my bearers gallantly gave an extra heave to the chair just in time to shake me back into the seat. Thanks to Martin's inimitable management the evening was, for me, an unforgettable success. A few weeks later, Judy Hutchinson also held a celebratory luncheon-party at Sarsden Glebe, Churchill, Oxfordshire, where it was good to see three dozen of our Oxfordshire friends, including John Schuster and colleagues from the Nuffield Orthopaedic Centre.

The day before our filming at Thames Television Studios the van developed a slipping clutch. We knew a shot of our arrival was planned, but did not expect such an array of cameras to be waiting as we drove up. The weather was perishingly cold and bronchitic tendencies were rearing their unwelcome heads. A producer approached us lovingly but firmly and, indicating my mother, asked me if she was able to reverse? Without referring to the clutch trouble I answered in the affirmative, at which he ordered us to go careering backwards and forwards from one given spot to another. His verdict was 'very good'; we hoped this would now lead us straight to the real thing, but he then disappeared indoors. An interval elapsed before someone opened the door of the van and asked if he might fumble with our clothing and, although by then my mother was fairly fed up with the whole performance, she allowed him to fiddle with her buttons and stuff her pockets full of wires. He then did the same to me, though we knew not for what reason. We waited for nearly an hour in the bitter whistling wind in an unheated car, nearly frozen, when at last the first tormentor reappeared, wiping his whiskers and obviously full of hot coffee. This time he directed our van to extremely difficult spots to improve the possible camera shots; understandably, my mother's patience was fast running out. Suddenly she said to me, with feeling: 'Not one of these silly buggers seems to have the least idea of what he is doing!' The purpose of the wires in our pockets had just dawned on me and I froze as I realised that her heartfelt message would go straight to the control room. The effect was immediate and, as if a ferret had entered a rabbit warren, the place was suddenly teeming with new faces and plans for action.

Once allowed to disembark, we were taken indoors to a cosy conference room where we were given coffee, thoughtfully laced with resuscitating brandy. After that the studio held no fears for us. With Mary Parkinson as our interviewer all was pleasant and friendly. My mother tells me that she quite forgot anyone was watching us; not surprisingly her performance was considered very natural. Later, we brushed cheeks with the senior studio personnel over a glass of wine and were heartily congratulated on our 'faultless' performance. A few days later that day's cold wind took its toll and drove me back to hospital; I was still there, when the programme went on screen. Geoffrey Spencer watched from behind my chair, and told me that from the sound of my voice I should not have been filming at all but been in hospital.

They discharged me just in time to order my hat for the Investiture. Through Mark Elwes' efforts a BBC Nationwide team turned up to interview us before and after. They called the previous day to warn us and I was grateful when my mother reluctantly agreed to be seen both on leaving for the Palace and returning home. Even so, when next morning she went in her petticoat to fetch the milk from outside our door, she was a bit taken aback to find several BBC men there already. They later took a stunning shot of her pushing me over Pembroke Road and it soon became clear that their main interest was in her age and my van. The crew were kindly, brisk and businesslike in interviewing me, then drove off ahead of us to the Palace, determined to get another close-up of the van as we drove in. We parted company – temporarily – at the gates.

The Royal entourage displayed its customary consideration and help for disabled people and left me amazed that amongst so many others who required to be welcomed to the Palace in orderly fashion, such individual attention was given to bores in chairs. A much more talented wheelchair occupant was also receiving an award – that brilliant cellist, Jacqueline du Pré. Our chairs were placed side by side at a good vantage point, which gave us an excellent view of the other presentees as they approached the starting gate. Several broke ranks to tell my neighbour how honoured they were to be invested on the same day as such a superb musician. I was beginning to feel a bit left out of it when a lady stopped to say, 'Oh, we did like you and your mother with Mary Parkinson!' That was a comfort. At the appointed time a splendid footman, called Paul, wheeled me to Her Majesty who invested me with my Order of the British Empire and expressed her sympathy and understanding of my condition.

Once outside we headed for Constitution Hill, where the BBC van was waiting patiently with microphone and cameras; there was also a bouquet of carnations for me. While we paused for a short interview, my mother's arm was hooked by two tourists from South Africa who wished her to pose with them for photographs to send home, but she evaded them. For the next two years, wherever we went in the van – sometimes even without it – we were accosted by complete strangers to say they had seen us on television. Some were just intrigued by the van, but others were incredibly flattering. Our biggest 'bag' occurred one morning in Peter Jones, where three separate individuals sprang out to say their piece from the glass, coats, and gifts departments respectively, as well as another who hailed my mother at the button counter. It was a revelation to us not only to find that so many watched television in the afternoon but that they remembered what they had seen.

Long after I had planned not to take on more in the disability field, I was seduced by the Handicapped Adventure Playground Association and joined its Executive Committee. The scheme was the brainchild of a remarkable educationalist called Lady Allen. She contrived to set up the first of these playgrounds in the beautiful rectory gardens of Old Church Street, Chelsea, where both physically and mentally retarded children have a wonderful time on the slides and swings, feeding the pet rabbits, or just messing around in muddy water with sticks and a raft. Increased confidence soon showed how much the children gained from having this new outlet for their previously confined spirits. I was reminded of my earlier days when, despite the best attempts of all, there were times when I sat wretchedly in the drawing-room, hearing the shouts and fun outside. These playgrounds were designed to be used and enjoyed by people in wheelchairs and with crutches, using sticks or wearing appliances. Three more playgrounds have been opened in Wandsworth, Islington and Fulham, and plans are being developed for other sites.

I was conscious of having done little to help the HAPA committee while other dedicated members had worked like Trojans, and for this reason I twice tried to resign, without success. Then, however, Clarissa Smith came to my rescue. Known as 'Click', Clarissa is a qualified teacher of speech and drama, and a children's entertainer, as well as being the youngest daughter of my Yorkshire friends from Barkston Ash, Geoffrey and Rosamond Smith. She promised me she would stage a children's show for HAPA on the Chelsea playground.

Click showed great dash and energy, aiming to popularise the HAPA concept with badges and tee-shirts. She decided to call the event the HAPA HOP and that it should have a Winnie the Pooh theme. She managed to persuade the actor, Christopher Biggins, to take the title rôle of Winnie the Pooh. On a boiling hot day he attended in full costume, to draw a raffle – prizes included a giant bear, Piglet, Tigger, Eeyore, pots of honey and lots more from that magic world. Click involved friends and contemporaries in the early twenties age group and successfully galvanised them into remarkable activity. The invitations were based on Winnie's way of doing-things-a-funny-way-round, so admission charges were set at: 'Children £1. Big Ones half price.' We begged prizes from all over London and further afield, and Click drove me round in the van to collect them during her spare moments. Her efforts worked like a charm, children and parents poured in, stalls and tombola did a roaring trade and we made a profit of £500. She organised the same event the following year and, with more helpers, nearly doubled the takings.

I now craftily accepted Click's offers to drive me about wherever I needed to go – to parties, to meetings, and to those theatres where she contrived to get my wheelchair admitted. All this she crammed into her extremely hectic life. It was marvellous for my overworked mother and sister to have another person to assist with getting me out and about. Luckily, the same things often amused both Click and me, so life was enhanced. She inflicted me on her unsuspecting friends and I was astonished to find with what willingness these young people would share the huge frolic of life with an 'oldie' caged up in a wheelchair.

Once, having gathered in Kensington Gardens for a picnic at which banana sandwiches were on the menu, our appetites gave out. As some very earnest trainee runners passed us, Click took off to run beside them and offer them a sandwich. She discovered they were mostly very hungry and then found one who was actually a friend and who clasped her to his bosom before returning, with her, to join our party. Her researches on theatres enabled her to get me into an excellent place at the back of the gallery in The Criterion, at the back of the stalls in Her Majesty's, in a very awkward box to see *Side by Side by Sondheim*, and into several others, of which some should remain anonymous because we managed to evade the rigid and unreasonable G.L.C. fire regulations. The fire regulations are a good example of an earlier era when the hazards and difficulties caused for and by those of us who are disabled were little understood. This was proved in one theatre where I was allowed to remain only if hauled out of my chair and into a seat, thus making me into an immovable mountain instead of a pretty agile mover, while my wheelchair stood open and unoccupied beside me.

Mixed in with taking me to LBC, GLAD, HAPA and the IBA, Click was building up her own business. She dressed up to order in a variety of nursery rhyme and Beatrix Potter character costumes, in which rôles she enlivened children's parties. When a one-roomed flat with bathroom fell vacant on the groundfloor of Marlborough Court, I longed to buy it as a bolthole in case I should find the lift out of order when coming in late. Click immediately said she would take a half share and use it as headquarters for her career. This arrangement could not have suited me better. We decorated, furnished and fitted up the flat to take my electric bed and hoist, as well as to house Click's interviewees and mutual stray friends.

Click's real niche is as a director or instructor and she has already taken a theatrical company to entertain audiences in huts and halls on many of the outer isles of Scotland. I know that her dexterity and competence has proved invaluable in tidying up this book. Her marriage to Simon Mitchell is most happily arranged so that she can still pursue her funny, yet effective, career.

The first chairman of the IBA's Local London Radio Advisory Committee resigned from office and for eight solid months I was referred to as 'acting chairman'. It was a relief when at last the Authority took the daring step of appointing me chairman, their earlier reluctance apparently based solely on grounds of my health. With this position, my links with Capital Radio and LBC were greatly strengthened. Fortunately, my three minute weekly spot with LBC, which I now record from home, was not considered sufficiently important to disqualify me for office.

I listened to many hours of phone-ins and their results. One evening, a lady said she wanted to know just what her standard of living was meant to be? Inflation had compelled her to part with her car, her television, her telephone, and now she had given up marmalade on her bread. Three nights later a man rang in to say he had so much admired this woman's realistic and uncomplaining attitude that he would like her to allow him to pay for at least a year's supply of her marmalade. On a more serious note, one man spoke of his near despair in continuing to cope with his wife's post-stroke condition; four calls were immediately received offering him and his wife help and accommodation for a holiday break, daily visits and help with the household chores. Haphazard it may be, but this sort of instant response and attempt to alleviate stress is heartwarming and impressive.

My weekly broadcasts sometimes seem to wave a magic wand. I helped someone housebound with multiple sclerosis to find more clients for her telephone answering service; to get a disabled family reunited, to their huge satisfaction; to get a vacancy in a training college for a teenage girl of small stature – she would have been called, in my younger days, a dwarf – when her morale had sunk to zero as a result of being continually refused jobs because she was 'too small'; to pull strings to get a wheelchair repaired at once in an emergency. To my delight, LBC has loaned me a stereophonic recording unit, known in the trade as a UHER, which enables me to tape my piece at home, or to interview people *in situ* as they work to improve conditions for the disabled. Capital Radio has set up a network for helping those in trouble and their Helpline service forms an inspired new pattern of constructively helpful compassion via radio.

Not long ago someone who should have known better asked me how I eked out my time. It would have been cruel to snap back the absolute truth that: like many able-bodied people, my days are never long enough. They start when I ring through to my mother at 7.30 a.m., at which point she collects the mail, papers and milk; she then dresses herself, props me into an eating position and brings my breakfast on a tray. I go through my medical routine of using respirator, inhaler and breathing pills. Then I am ready for either Pooh or my mother to assume the role of physiotherapist, turning me on my side to smack and squeeze me over the ribs to remove any lurking foreign bodies. One or other then prepares to get me up.

My room has a festoon of electric wires from the powered bed, heater and blanket, as well as from the telephone. These have given my mother several falls, so when anyone telephones while she picks her way amongst them, or while she is fixing the slings under me to attach me to the hoist, the atmosphere is extremely tense. Many an unsuspecting caller at this stage of the proceedings has received a brusque dismissal. Once the hoist has safely planted me into the wheelchair, we move along to the bathroom where the electric hoist works excellently apart from its busy cacophony of sound which is more than enough to jar any frayed or fragile nerves. If this reads like a formidable routine, let me explain that probably the only reason why it does not particularly test or oppress us is that we understand each other, so can growl away without impairing our relationship more than temporarily. We dawdle a bit in the process of getting up, discussing the news and the changing scene so even with the help we receive from Pooh, the whole business takes about two and a half hours from the time my mother leaves her bed. Often during the night I guiltily summon my mother to change my position. The bell has been known to go wrong just when I urgently need to use my respirator and on those occasions I telephone to Pooh, who trips up the stairs like an angel of mercy.

For about twenty years well-wishers have confided to me, either gently or bluntly, that there really should be a clean break between me and my mother without delay. They never have an alternative to advance, so I am inclined to feel they see ours as an untidy arrangement which offends their inner eye. Had I followed their advice, I should have missed all these wonderful years. While I can't fool myself into believing the theory that it is by being so heavily committed to me that my mother has remained so astonishingly spry, at least it is a comforting fallacy. The truth is however, that she picks up admirers wherever she goes and has a remarkable grasp of the times, coupled with a flexibility and ability to accept change which have saved her from any bitterness about growing old and deaf. Her warm humanity, insatiable curiosity and quick repartee commend her to people of every generation and walk of life. Furthermore, she is devoid of jealousy; it is something she abhors.

To plan for a future in which I was alone could be superfluous, considering the uncertain prognosis for my condition. But if this has now to be done, it will be in very much better conditions than those obtaining twenty, or even ten, years ago. In the last ten years a battery of protective forces has emerged to surround disabled people and this caring atmosphere compares amazingly with the arid outlook of the 1930s. These better conditions have been brought about mostly through the stalwart endeavours of talented disabled people who have fought hard and long to get improvements: people like Mary Greaves, Sue Masham, Anne Armstrong, Peter Large, John Beckingham, Dick Learner, Robin Cavendish, Diana Law, Liz Fanshawe, John Bithell, Norman Croucher, David Hyde, Bob Miley, June Opie, John Prestwich, Jean Harvey, Robert Bowell, Stephen Bradshaw, Bert Massey, Selwyn Goldsmith, Nigel Harvey, Charles Pocock, Rosalie Wilkins and Nancy Robertson. Numbers of able-bodied people, too, devote large chunks of their lives to helping us. These include doctors and Members of Parliament who take up the cudgels on our behalf, while amongst others Lady Hamilton occupies a leading place. I consider Lady Hamilton's most important achievement has been to remind both the authorities and the manufacturers that they should cater for us in forward planning, and to have done so in such a painless way that this principle has become fashionable rather than a heavy burden.

In general, social services departments now expect to have to cope with us, though some do this better than others. There are employment agencies, rehabilitation and retraining units, and volunteer bodies directly concerned with us, such as the Disabled

Living Foundation, Disablement Income Group, Joint Committee on Mobility for the Disabled, Disabled Drivers' Motor Club, Disabled Drivers' Association, Association of Disabled Professionals, and many more. There is the increasing vigour of GLAD and the County Disablement Associations and the many societies relating to specific conditions, such as the Spastics Society, and groups to deal with cases of Rheumatism and Arthritis, Parkinson's Disease, Polio, Muscular Dystrophy, Huntington's Chorea, Multiple Sclerosis, Frederich's Ataxia, Myasthenia Gravis, Ileostomy, Spinal Injuries, Brittle Bones etc. In addition, we have the research organisations, sports and recreational bodies, and organisations that provide and develop the essential equipment to help blind and handicapped people to turn the pages of books, or to hear cassettes of books recorded by actors and good readers. The standard of holiday home and of residential accommodation, in most instances, has improved a great deal. There is still a dearth of establishments where people who wish to earn their own living can be both accommodated and provided with limited care to help them with dressing and putting to bed, to overcome the loss of home care on a regular basis. The Crossroads Scheme, which provides back-up support for families coping with disabled members, has proved a great success in its initial trial areas and extensions of it may well form a partial solution to the problem of severely disabled people to remain in their homes.

It would be too much to expect that in the growing popularity of the disablement cause there would not be a few sharks using their teeth to get a cut of our brighter fortunes. Such people can do a lot of harm because the feeling in favour of us is still precarious amongst the general public and can quickly turn into an unhelpful gut reaction, supporting the dyspeptic view that too much is being done for us. The situation is delicate and there is no room for arrogance, tactlessness and certainly not for dishonesty and corruption. Happily these flaws are far from prevalent, but even a trace of them is too much.

Obviously our main target must be to improve the scene for all who have to live their lives at reduced capacity. There is now a very welcome attitude of encouraging everyone to live out their earthly existence as fully as possible given the co-operation of the rest of society, and this makes a change from the time when it was regarded almost as a privilege for wheelchair-bound people to be able to move around in public.

It may be attractive to watch the more beautiful and elegant of the able-bodied use the world as their plaything, but it can be nauseating if they restrict their interests and endeavours to the sole use of themselves and their offspring. They are the ones who choose to ignore the real handicap of disability until something happens to them. Either they do not care or cannot imagine how much it hurts to be physically prevented from getting on in the world and to be faced by endless disappointments. Fortunately, there are others who have an innate understanding of how to help, though they themselves are not disabled. These are the ones who know that it is not enough just to ring and enquire after our health, whereas that it is a great help to do something positive, like endeavouring to include us in parties or celebrations, despite our uncouth appearance and probable inability to attend.

It is a misconception that a multitude of organisations necessarily streamlines the work to be done; often it does not, and neither do pious words from the Government always turn into cash. Every ounce of benefit must be squeezed from money given for the disability cause, whether by a mainly generous public or by a fairly parsimonious Government. Funds inevitably are limited and must be garnered scrupulously, spent only with full consideration of the whole scene and with the minimum of bad planning and overlap. Some ventures should be firmly discouraged. It has been suggested to me that as a means of husbanding resources, a Minister for the Disabled, preferably with a well-disposed Secretary of State for Social Services, should keep every organisation under constant review and publicly accountable for its actions. So far Alfred Morris M.P. has been the one and only Minister for the Disabled and everyone recognises his deep and sincere dedication to furthering our interests. Nevertheless sometimes even his endeavours have amounted to no more than the soothing words of a Government public relations exercise, because his Parliamentary powers are weak since he does not have a seat in the Cabinet. It is at Cabinet level that important decisions are made and it may be that our case would be better served in future if dealt with by the Cabinet Ministers responsible for the Treasury, Social Services, Employment, Housing, Education, Environment and other departments, each doing their bit to integrate disabled people into the community.

The mobility scheme is still a bone of contention in many respects, but to have it at all is a triumph. Much credit must go to the Joint Committee on Mobility, whose reasoned arguments helped to get payments increased from £4 per week on 1st January 1976, to £10 in July 1978. The pity is that when the invalid 'trike' ceased to be issued on grounds of safety and unsuitability, no alternative vehicle was found to replace it, so disabled school leavers are left with no means of transport by which to continue their education or find work; for them no mobility allowance can replace the independence of the 'trike'. Older people are shoved aside in the scramble for younger groups to get the allowance, no matter how severely they are disabled nor over how long a period they have suffered their disability. The injustice of this system based on longevity becomes still more flagrant when compared with the free or concessionary fares now awarded to able-bodied pensioners on public transport which cannot be used by handicapped people because of their disabilities. Any glaring anomaly or injustice is an embarrassment to administrators and negotiators who aim to increase an allowance and to ensure that all who receive it will not fall behind, but in the case of elderly disabled people this disqualification from the mobility allowance deserves priority attention.

In a strange way, public provision either overdoes it and caters for us as though we must have the most expensive possible amenity, or else fails to recognise our existence. For instance, some building provision for us is more elaborate than necessary, yet many kerbs at road intersections are not ramped to allow us to cross the road as ordinary members of society. We do not want to be unduly coddled but do want the chance to be useful – at least, I *think* we want to be, and if we are not prepared to accept the responsibility that goes with independence, we would be better off in residential accommodation. There is no doubt whatever that to get a splint or wheelchair repaired, to get details of all available benefits and, most important of all, to get understanding help towards satisfactory employment, a disabled person has to battle relentlessly. Inevitably, the number of snubs and disappointments handed out to disabled people by low, and medium-grade civil servants is greater than the general public would ever credit, an irony which calls for a little applied psychology in areas where red tape has gone mad.

A great deal now is talked about 'attitudes'. We hear a lot about improving attitudes in the community to accept disabled people more readily, but there is another side to the coin. There are thoughtless people in wheelchairs and on crutches who actually refuse assistance when it is offered to them. I can see very little excuse for not being civil and, if possible, grateful whenever help is offered; the would-be helper has probably overcome embarrassment to make the offer and should be dealt with appreciatively at all costs, if only to ensure that next time they come upon one of us (who may be less articulate than some) they are not then frightened to give us a hand. I am irritated by my disabled colleagues when I hear them cast aside good help as though it were dross. Arrogance in any form is wholly inappropriate, as is all behaviour which detracts from the common courtesy that should exist among people.

Occasionally, a disabled person who has been battered and embittered by life points an accusing finger at me and wags it, telling me that I don't know how lucky I am. There he is completely wrong, because I do. Probably I know that I am still more lucky than he suspects because of my hospital experience. I have learnt there that if you can possibly summon up the strength to be reasonably lighthearted, you get better help and co-operation from both staff and fellow patients. If you can laugh your way out of trouble the world is on your side, so my advice is to try and put on a bit of an act. When I have found fellow patients whose spirits are at a low ebb, I have suggested this method and those who try it often appear to improve dramatically. At these times I am reminded of Pat Leahy's theories, preached in the 1930s. In hospital, there is a barrier of fear the overcoming of which is not exactly helped by the traditional pomposity exercised by some members of the medical profession; on Phipps Ward there is no such pomposity. Geoffrey Spencer treats each patient as his equal and in return gets remarkable results, often from dismal beginnings. No doubt there are doctors who cannot translate their learned views into lay terms for the benefit of their patients, many of whom must be both trying and inconsiderate in their search for the facts; but knowing the good effects achieved by the open, modern method used on Phipps Ward, I believe that in other hospital wards, the less communicative doctors there should have an interpreter, trained in psychology, to forge a link with their seriously afflicted patients. Without the co-operation that stems from understanding, the natural healing processes must be denied a great deal of their recuperative power.

A medical spokesman of some authority recently warned a meeting of social workers and therapists that all disabled adults at some time are sure to ask the question: 'Why me?' I was present, and longed to tell her that in my case she was wrong; moreover, I knew of others like me who never bothered their heads with such sterile nonsense. It is our good luck to have the ability to accept disability as one of the horrors meted out in this enigmatic existence, yet also to recognise that ours is far from the only trouble in the world. We are privileged to have this outlook, which generally results from having been nurtured in families whose philosophy is to take the rough with the smooth, without complaining unduly. For me, perhaps, above everything it is my insatiable interest in the small events of everyday existence that preserves me from speculating on 'what might have been.'

It would be stupid and oafish to try to describe what I owe to my family and real friends. I should like to give them a resounding burst of applause but that is not possible because my unco-operative shoulder muscles will not allow me to clap my hands! My debt of gratitude is in a currency beyond repayment, which is lucky for me.